What To Do When You Become
THE BOSS

How new managers
become successful managers

BOB SELDEN
With Foreword by Dennis Pratt

Outskirts Press, Inc.
Denver, Colorado

What To Do When You Become The Boss
How new managers become successful

Illustrations by Peter Burleigh © 2008

Outskirts Press, Inc.
http://www.outskirtspress.com

ISBN: 978-1-4327-1428-4

Outskirts Press and the "OP" logo are trademarks belonging to Outskirts Press, Inc.

PRINTED IN THE UNITED STATES OF AMERICA

Testimonials

"Intuitive, informative, and insightful discussions of what to do (and what not) when you become the boss. As I read, I was reminded of how important it is to understand the dynamics when managing your team, your boss, your peers and last but not least, yourself. This book is packed with excellent advice. It's an invaluable resource for those about to join the league of managers. Actually, it's an invaluable resource for everyone in management."

Martin P. J. John, Pigments & Additives Division, Head of Marketing & Sales Support, Clariant International Ltd, Switzerland

"A fabulous book! Whatever the industry or profession, this book is invaluable to the new manager. Working in a foreign country tasked with capacity building is challenging and it's not always easy to focus on the training and transfer of skills and knowledge. This book has made me realise the importance of empowering people and provided me with useful insights on motivating those I supervise and work with. Structured according to the reader's learning style, this book engages the reader and covers relevant topics in an easy to read format."

Maria José Campos, Senior Legal Officer, Timor Sea Designated Authority, Dili, Timor

"I have been working with Bob for some time now and his advice has always been insightful, practical and effective. His book is just as good! I wish I had a copy of it when I first became a manager 10 years ago. I would have done much better in many areas. Get a copy and keep it close to you in the office. It will be one of your best investments, ever."

Luciano Almeida de Jesus, Head of Risk Management & Performance Measurement, ING Investment Management Europe, The Hague, The Netherlands

Contents

Foreword

By Dennis Pratt

Today, as I write this, it is my birthday. It is 48 years to the day since I was appointed to my first managerial position. I became leading hand 'over' fourteen tradesmen I had been an apprentice 'under' six weeks before.

Some months before then I had passed an aircraft maintenance engineers licence test and just about everybody else had failed it. A Licensed Aircraft Maintenance Engineer had to be at least 21, so I couldn't be granted the license until my twenty-first birthday. On that day, on the basis that I had correctly answered a lot of questions about aeroplanes, I was appointed to a position where I was supposed to be managing people.

It was a baptism of fire. I made many mistakes. But I was lucky. My foreman Jack was a wise old leader and manager who advised and coached me in my job as leading hand. He saved me many times when I did things that caused problems within my team, and he used each of my errors to help me learn. I was reminded of Jack's many words of wisdom as I read through the draft chapters of this book.

In this book, Bob tells a similar story to mine about a boss who coached and guided him in his early days as a manager. (See the chapter on appraisals and his story about Kendall.) We were both incredibly lucky to have found ourselves with bosses like that. Despite the many years since Bob and I were thrown in at the deep end, and despite the many management books and articles warning that managerial appointments shouldn't be made on technical skills alone, most new managers are still appointed today because they are technically competent. Little thought is given to how they will cope with managing and leading their team of people.

I say "most" new managers are appointed because they are technically competent purely on the basis of forty years experience consulting to very many organisations. Over that time I have seen little change in the process of appointing new managers. Very few that I have seen have been put through a program of development into their new job of "getting things done through other people". And only the lucky ones get a Jack or a Kendall to help them through their early years of trial and error learning.

Jack helped me and corrected my managerial actions when he saw me doing something that he thought I could have done better. But he couldn't watch me all the time, and some things about managing aren't all that visible anyhow. So there were things about managing and leading that I had to learn after I had moved on from under Jack's protective wing. (After several years of this, I decided that I was a better operator than I was leader or manager, so I became a consultant.)

The book you are about to read fills the role of the helpful boss like Jack and Kendall. Because it is the accumulated wisdom of the many years Bob has spent managing and observing other managers, it provides the new manager with advice and guidance in a lot more areas than could be done by one helpful boss. (You usually have to make a mistake before your boss explains how you should have done it. This book tells you how not to make mistakes in all the critical areas of leading and managing.)

I met Bob in 1979 when we worked together at United Permanent Building Society. He was then and remains today the most professional trainer of people in organisations I have met. His approach to helping people learn is evident all the way through this book. (Only a professional trainer would start out by asking you to look at your own learning style and then guide you through each topic in the book according to the way you learn and absorb information.)

This book is an easy read, with most of the information presented in bite-sized chunks. It is a dip-innable book – you don't have to start at the beginning and work all the way through it. (You don't have to, but I certainly recommend that you do read it all the way through.) The important thing is that, like the helpful boss, this book is there to provide advice on each area of managing when you need that advice.

For the 'helpful boss' who has a new manager in a reporting relationship, this book can help you develop your new person. You can discuss the chapter headings with your new person, then guide him or her to read those areas where development is required, and discuss them with you.

While Bob has written the book primarily for the new manager, I believe the advice is every bit as useful for many managers with years of experience. Each managerial position calls for some people-managing skills but very few call for all the skills covered in this book. Managers moving from one job to another should find helpful advice in this book when adapting to their new position.

And then, there may be people who read this book and decide that the whole idea of managing and leading other people is not for them. I reckon that is a legitimate decision. (I have to believe that, it's the decision I took about my own career.) Fortunately there are many organisations today, especially in the high-tech and finance areas, where it is recognised that career paths can permit people to become high-level operators and technicians without having to move into managerial or leadership positions in order to get promotion.

So, read on.

Introduction

How do you want to use this book?

Training courses! *His most recent had been termed "Management for Senior Officers" and had been a minor disaster – all psychology and how to be nice to junior officers. How to **involve** them, how to **motivate** them, how to **relate** to them. Inspector John Rebus had returned to his station and tried it for one day, a day of involving, of motivating, of relating. At the end of the day, a Detective Constable had slapped a hand on Rebus' back, smiling.*

"Bloody hard work today, John. But I've enjoyed it."

"Take your hand off my fu...ng back." Rebus had snarled. "And don't call me John."

The DC's mouth fell open. "But you said ..." he began, but didn't bother finishing. The brief holiday was over. Rebus had tried being a manager. Tried it and loathed it. (From "Tooth and Nail", by Ian Rankin, St. Martin's Paperbacks, 1996, New York)

Perhaps you too are a little like Ian Rankin's Inspector John Rebus, who found it difficult to learn to be a manager. If so, you'll find some good news in this book.

Important - read this!

The difficulty with learning how to be a manager is probably not to do with "management" itself. Rather, it's usually the way the learning is presented to us and the different ways in which we prefer to learn. If you've ever been to a training course or seminar that you found boring or unsuited to you, then you can probably relate to Rebus' experience.

This book will make learning to be a manager easier for you and more enjoyable. The book can be used in different ways by a variety of people. It can fit your personal learning style.

But please read on before you are tempted to jump to Chapter One!

Each of us learns in a different way and at a different pace. Researchers suggest that in general we have a preference for learning through seeing, learning through listening, or learning through moving, doing and touching.

Peter Honey and Alan Mumford (www.peterhoney.com) have developed four main learning styles that they call "learning preferences". Read through them and tick all the statements that are most like you – this will give you an indication of your preferred learning style. This book is designed to recognise your preferred style so that you can easily (and sometimes quickly) navigate your way to the best parts.

Let's start. Remember, tick all of the following statements which appear **most** like you.

What's your preferred style of learning?

Activist
☐ Are you always looking for new experiences?
☐ Are you open minded and enthusiastic about new ideas but get bored with the implementation of them?
☐ Are you always on the go and enjoy doing things – do you often tend to act first and consider the implications afterwards?
☐ Do you like working with others but tend to hog the limelight? (Be honest, no one is looking, remember it said "tend to …")

Reflector
☐ Do you like to stand back and look at a situation from different perspectives before taking action?
☐ Do you like to collect data and think about it carefully before coming to any conclusions?
☐ Do you enjoy observing others and listening to others' views before offering your own?
☐ Do you like to be given plenty of notice or warning before you have to make a decision?

Theorist
☐ Do you like to adapt and integrate your observations into (sometimes) complex and logically sound theories? (only Theorists will understand that statement)
☐ Do you often think problems through in a step by step way?
☐ Do you tend to be a perfectionist who likes to fit things into a rational scheme?
☐ Do you sometimes appear to others as being detached and analytical rather than subjective or emotive in your thinking?

Pragmatist
☐ Are you keen to try things out?.
☐ Do you look for concepts or models that can be applied to your job.?
☐ Do you tend to be impatient with lengthy discussions?
☐ Would others describe you as "practical and down to earth"?

Which is your preferred style of learning?

Read the descriptions over again, then make a note of the description that best suits the way you prefer to learn. Is your learning style more of a **Pragmatist, Theorist, Reflector** or **Activist?** You may find that there are two styles you relate to – that's OK, you can take a bit of both. For example, your learning style might be '**Pragmatic Reflector**'.

Once you have established your preferred learning style, you can then use this book in four different ways, or if you like, a combination of ways.

Let's jump in . . .

ACTIVISTS – how to get the most out of this book	
If your preferred style of learning is mainly similar to the Activist . . .	**Why?**
1 Chances are by now, you're getting bored with this discussion.	Hang in there! Take heart, there are some short cuts made for you. You won't have to read this book from cover to cover. In fact, you'll be directed to the parts that are best for you - the action parts are found at the end of each chapter.
2 Buy another copy of this book straight away.	Give it to a colleague who has a similar Activist style to you. Arrange to meet him or her in a week's time to discuss how the two of you will get the best out of this book.
3 Talk with your colleague about how he/she has managed difficult management situations.	Invite your colleague to lunch for a discussion about how to manage difficult situations.
4 Make an appointment to meet with your colleague for lunch once a month for the next six months to discuss your learning results.	Of course if you do this, you probably won't need to read any further.

Some general learning tips for **Activists** (other than using this book):

- Get involved in project teams – particularly at the start of the project. Volunteer for the brainstorming or idea generation segments, but not for implementation issues or activities. It's a good idea to take on the Chair's role so that you can direct others.

- Visit other organisations to see how they do things (short visits only).
- Take part in business games.
- Avoid conferences or training courses where you know there will be a lot of theory presentations. If you have to attend, make sure you ask a lot of questions to keep yourself from being bored. Try to take a lot of notes or draw pictures during the "boring" presentation parts. Think about how the issues being raised could be used back at work.
- Right now, take a quick look at the PS at the end of this introduction. Then, go straight to the Introduction to *Part 1: Leading and Managing* for your next steps – you won't need to read any more of this introduction.

REFLECTORS – how to get the most out of this book	

If your preferred style of learning is mainly similar to the Reflector . . .	Why?
1 Keep reading – this will be interesting for you.	Read through the remainder of this introduction so that you can come to some sound decisions about using this book.
2 Revisit the description of styles.	Make sure you are happy with your decision as a Reflector.
3 Buy another copy of this book straight away.	Give it to a colleague who has a similar Reflector style to you. After you have read through this introduction, then Chapters One and Two and completed the Managerial Time Log mentioned there, arrange to meet with your colleague to compare time logs.
4 Think and take notes as you read.	There's a lot to think about in this book, so you will need to take notes as you progress and keep copies of the activities and exercises to discuss with your colleague.

Some general learning tips for **Reflectors** (other than using this book):

- Take the time to watch people as they work – particularly in groups; watch how they respond to one another.
- When you have just been through a difficult experience, take some time off (an hour or two) to think about it. Write down what went right, what went wrong and what you would do differently next time.
- At least once a year, take a day or so off work and spend your time reflecting on what has gone and what you need to do over the coming 12 months to improve. Try to split your reflection time between 20% reflecting on the past and 80% focusing on what you are going to do in the coming 12 months.

THEORISTS – how to get the most out of this book	
If your preferred style of learning is mainly similar to the Theorist. . .	**Why?**
1 Keep reading.	Throughout this book there are plenty of concepts, theories and models to think about and apply.
2 Buy another copy of this book straight away. Seek out a colleague who has a similar learning style to yours.	Arrange to meet with him/her regularly – every fortnight would be ideal. Make sure that the meetings are well structured, they have clear aims and are based around a particular management challenge, concept or theory outlined in this book (in fact later in the book you'll see how these meetings can be structured).
3 Take particular note of the sections in this book that have to do with people's feelings.	As a manager, these types of activities could be described as your blind spots, so it is particularly important to focus on these.
4 It will be useful for you to run a training session or meeting with your team around one of the key concepts in this book.	Explaining the concept to others will force you to think about how best it could work in practice.

Some general learning tips for **Theorists** (other than using this book):

- Undertake training courses and activities that are highly structured. You will need to make sure that the training is based on sound logic and reasoning and contains interesting concepts.
- Because you are less likely to attend courses of an emotive or feeling nature, go out of your way to do so. Keep in mind the above point so that they won't be too painful for you.
- Watch for management development articles (The Harvard Business Review is an excellent source). Send a copy of an article to colleagues who think similarly to yourself – ask them to read it and attach three or four questions that you think are relevant to your workplace. Ask for their feedback. If you really want to get into a management topic in depth, the publication "Organizational Dynamics" is very good. Remember to always ask "How can this work in my situation?"
- Seek out interesting projects where the issues are complex.
- Set yourself up as an expert in a particular field of your work and encourage others to ask for your advice. Be careful to see how the issues they raise relate to how you might also improve your own management style and behaviour.

PRAGMATISTS – how to get the most out of this book	
If your preferred style of learning is mainly similar to the Pragmatist . . .	**Why?**
1 Apologies for taking so long to get to you.	For the rest of the book the key concepts will be highlighted for you and you'll be directed to them ASAP
2 No, you don't have to buy another copy of this book (but if you find you like it, please pass it on to a friend).	In the meantime, find another manager whom you respect and who is recognised as an effective manager.
3 When you have an issue at work, or this book raises a particular management challenge, seek out your colleague and ask him/her how they would handle it.	Invite your colleague to lunch for a discussion about how to manage difficult situations.
4 If you have had a performance review recently, or better still 360 degree feedback, pull the results out now and review them. What are the two or three areas where you need to develop most?	Keep these in mind as you go through the rest of this book so that you can apply the practical tips and techniques to your own situation.

Some general learning tips for **Pragmatists** (other than using this book):

- Look for training courses that have a particular relevance to your industry and job. Make sure they include plenty of feedback (such as 360 degree profiles, role plays and active coaching from the trainer).
- Look for management techniques – e.g. principles, concepts, techniques that will save you time.
- Look for management models. Ask some of your colleagues (such as the Theorists) to show you how the "best management concepts they know" work in practice.
- Avoid theory type training sessions, meetings and books. If you buy a management book, make sure it has lots of "How to". At the end of most of the chapters in this book there is an "How to implement the ideas in this chapter straight away" section. You will really find this

practical, quick and useful.

- Look for training DVDs that show you "How to", but do not dwell on theory.
- Get a trusted colleague to sit in on some of your management meetings and give you some feedback on their effectiveness. Make sure to ask him/her how they would run them if they were you.

And so…

Does management training have to be painful? The old saying of "no pain, no gain" should **not** apply to learning about how to be a better manager! Management training should be interesting, fun - even exciting - and it can be that way for you when it is designed to suit your particular learning style.

At least some of the above tips on learning about management will prove useful – mix and match to suit your own preferred style of learning. It would be sad to think that we might all end up like John Rebus, loathing being a manager simply because we do not have the right opportunities to learn.

Good luck with learning to be a manager.

By the way - to all you Activists who read this far without jumping straight to Chapter One, well done!

P.S. Chapters One and Two in Section One are compulsory reading (but there are some tips on how to get through them quickly if this is an aspect of your learning preference). Then you're free to roam wherever you like throughout the book according to your need and style. The book is laid out in five sections so you can find your topic easily:

1. **Leading and Managing**
   So, now you're in charge of other people. Where do you start?

2. **Managing Your Team**
   They've given you a team. Now what do you do?

3. **Managing Upwards and Sideways**
   How do you get things done when you have no formal control?

4. **Managing Your Meetings**
   One-on-one is ok, but how do you influence people in groups?

5. **Managing Yourself**
   How do you get the best out of yourself?

All the best with learning to become a manager.

Bob Selden

Part 1: Leading and Managing

So, now you're in charge of other people. Where do you start?

Becoming a manager for the first time can be a scary experience. I was very lucky. I only had two people to manage – a young, in-experienced but bright young man and a very experienced, older lady. In terms of experience, in these two I had the two extremes. I was also lucky that they were both very motivated. So, my role became one of trainer for the young gun and supporter for the older, more experienced lady. After 18 months I moved to my next role, which you could say was my first real challenge as a manager – 10 people to manage, all far more experienced (technically) than me and most thought they should have my job.

What's your current challenge as a manager? To help you focus for this first part of the book:

- Think about the three things that challenge you most in your new role.
- What are they?
- Keep these in mind as you read through Part 1 so that you can relate your own situation to the examples and guidelines given.

In this first part of the book, the aim is to provide you with:

- A clear distinction between managing and leading. This distinction will en-able you to focus straight away on achieving the results required of you as a manager by the organisation. It will also provide you with guidance to gradually build and develop your leadership skills (leadership takes just a little more time to develop).

- A pro-forma action plan that you can fill in and follow as you progress in your role over the next six months. This will enable you to put into practise immediately some of the ideas that you find useful in the first two chapters.

For **Activists** to help you through Chapters One and Two:

- Go straight to the "How to implement the ideas in this chapter" at the end of Chapters One and Two. See what your action plan might look like for the next few months.
- Then, find a good colleague with whom you can discuss Chapter One.
- Finally, go through Chapter One and read as much as you can. The concept of the manager's role having three elements - Leading, Managing and Operating will be vital for your success. Discuss these with your colleague to get the full implication. Repeat the above process for Chapter Two.

For **Pragmatists**:

- Skim point 4 *"The things leaders do that encourage others to follow them?"* and point 5 *"You may be thinking, Well, how can I become a leader?"* in Chapter One. This will give you an overview of the concept of how leaders can create the conditions that will encourage others to follow.
- Go back to the start of Chapter One and commence reading. Chapter Two builds nicely on the key concepts outlined in Chapter One.

Theorists and **Reflectors:** Read on and enjoy!

Chapter 1

Are You a Leader or a Manager?

1. You as a *Leader*– the first element of the Manager's Role

The case of James and his new role

James took over as the new Plant Manager for a bio tech factory where he would be managing approximately 400 people. Prior to his arrival, there was an "Ask Gavin" column (Gavin was the previous Plant Manager) on the site intranet. Employees could pose their questions and get answers – they could either give their name or remain anonymous.

On the surface, this sounded like a good idea. However, nothing substitutes for face to face communication. People rarely use such vehicles to ask the difficult questions and if they do, they almost never give their name. One of the first changes James made, was to change the title of this communication channel to "Ask Management". Why? In his wanderings around the site, James had got the distinct impression that his predecessor had ruled as "My way is the only way". Consequently, the intranet communication channel was rarely used. So, James also wanted to distance himself from the previous manager.

Two weeks into the job, the monthly site meeting took place where all employees gathered in the cafeteria to be briefed by management. It was the expectation at these meetings that new managers would introduce themselves and give their new colleagues some background about their experience and work history. When the facilitator turned to James as the new head of the plant and asked would he like to introduce himself, James stood up and asked:

"Would Francene Dante please stand up?"

You can imagine the hushed silence that greeted James! Could you imagine being Francene? She was sinking lower into her chair. Then, slowly at first, but then more frantically, Francene's work colleagues en-

couraged her to stand. As she did so, James said:

"Francene, I would like to thank you very much for giving your name when you asked a question on the intranet Ask Management. I know you didn't have to, but I very much appreciate that you did. You see, I value honesty, integrity and sincerity and I like to be able to communicate freely with everyone on the site and they should feel the same about talking with me. So, thank you once again most sincerely"

"That's who I am."

James then sat down.

What impact do you think this one action of James' had? Most of us as new managers would probably have done the usual thing at the site meeting when asked to introduce ourselves. We would have given a brief overview of our work history and maybe a bit about ourselves as a person (I know I would).

James immediately set himself apart as a leader. He decided to take some action that would demonstrate three of his core values – honesty, sincerity and integrity. The old saying that "actions speak louder than words", was never truer than in James' case. He also wanted to demonstrate that communication is a two way process. Merely talking about it would not have achieved the results he achieved with his one action.

James very clearly, was displaying some of the best facets of the **leading** element of his new managerial role.

In fact there are three elements of all manager's roles:

Leading	*Managing*	*Operating*

"Roles" may be formally described by an organisation as 'manager', 'supervisor', 'leading hand', 'director' and so on - these are roles where somebody is accountable for the work of other people as well as his or her own work.

Whatever your own managerial role may be called, it will contain an element of:

- leading,
- managing, and
- operating.

Managing and **operating** are covered in Chapter Two. First, to **leading**.

2. Is there a difference between a *leader* and a *manager*? Can you be both? Do you need to be both?

By the way, before answering these questions, let me fill you in on what James told me was a really nice outcome from his introductory speech. In the few days following the site meeting, he said he had many more people taking the time to talk to him at lunch in the cafeteria or as he passed their work stations, than he had in his previous two weeks at the plant. He also received many emails from people giving their names and apologising for not giving their names in previous questions to "Ask Management".

Almost 100 years ago, Mary Parker Follett described a manager as "One who gets things done through people". This description is still used by management educators and scholars today. However, this should now be enhanced to read:

"One who gets the things the organisation requires the manager to get done, through the people who report to that manager"

There are two reasons for suggesting these additions:

- You automatically become a **manager** when you **sign on for the job**
- You only become a **leader** when **your people say so**

You are given the title of "manager" by the organisation. People will do things for you, either well or not so well depending on how well you manage them, because of WHAT you are not WHO you are.

Only your people, your team, the people you manage, can give you the title of "leader".

Another way of putting it is to say that the organisation gives you your "corporate" manager's hat when you sign on. This lets everyone in the organisation know that you are now officially a manager. Then, your people, when they believe in you and only when they believe in you and are prepared to follow you, give you your leadership badge, your badge of honour!

Let me make a very important point. Managing can be described as more mechanical and so there are guidelines to follow, whereas leading is always measured through others' perceptions.

In this book, I will describe many techniques and provide you with guidelines for becoming a better manager. If you follow the suggestions, I can guarantee that you will become a better manager. I will also give you some pointers for developing yourself as a leader. However, it will be up to your people to decide how well you have followed these.

Here's a quick way of checking your current leadership status.

Once you have been in your current role for say, nine to twelve months, ask yourself:

☐ *"Would my people do the things I now ask them to do even if I were not their manager?"*

☐ *If you can truthfully answer "Yes", then you are well on the path to becoming a leader.*

Many of you will probably answer this with a "Maybe". Try not to be concerned at this, as the road to leadership is a long one, but a truly rewarding one. If you are concerned that it seems to be taking you forever to develop as a leader, keep in mind the experience of one of the greatest leaders of our time, Nelson Mandela who spent 27 years in prison waiting to show how he could lead his country!

James, the plant manager who was mentioned earlier, not only demonstrated his leadership skills quickly, but also has a very clear understanding of the distinction between management and leadership. He has renamed the top team of the plant (the committee of senior managers that make the plant decisions) from "The Leadership Team" to "The Management Team". Food for thought …

3. Are leaders born or made? Can I become a leader?

It might be reasonable to assume that leadership can be developed. However, there has been and still is, considerable debate on the issue. Even the experts are divided. To help answer this, it's first necessary to look at what makes a leader a "leader" - then we might be able to see whether leadership can be learnt.

A colleague, Professor Preston Bottger who is Professor of Leadership at the International Institute for Management Development in Switzerland, tells the story of when he was asked by his eight year old daughter's teacher to address her school class on leadership.

"How do you talk to eight year olds about leadership?" he said. So, being a professor, he asked the class the obvious question:

"Who can tell me what a leader is?"

Straight away a boy in the front row put up his hand:

"A leader does things first", he enthused.

His response was quickly followed by an equally enthusiastic girl who said:

"Leaders have followers".

Could the experts give us any better answers than those? – "Leaders do things first"; and "Leaders have followers".

Using the definition of leadership these children gave Preston, do you know any people whom you might call leaders?

Often when people are asked this question, they respond with the names of famous historical leaders such as Gandhi, Kennedy, Churchill and more recently, Mandela. Chances are however, you've personally been greatly influenced by people around you who display leadership, but whom you've not credited or thought of, as leaders before. For example, parents, siblings, teachers, managers and colleagues who have acted as role models for you and whose advice you have followed from time to time. In fact, we generally only think of these people as leaders well after they have had an influence on us.

Think for a moment about the famous world leaders that now come to mind when you are asked to name leaders. Now, compare them to some of the people who have had a major impact on you personally. It's likely that these two groups share many of the same qualities, but more importantly, they actually do many of the same things.

What are these "things" that leaders do that set them apart from others? Can you too learn how to do them?

4. The *four things leaders do* that encourage others to follow

Leaders become leaders because they do at least four things for us that make us inclined to follow them:

LEADERS DO FOUR THINGS . . .	*That encourage others to follow . . .*
1. **They help us understand and make sense of our environment.**	So for example, when things aren't working out or are unclear for us, they are able to explain what is happening in practical terms that we can understand.
2. **They help give us a sense of direction.**	They are able to paint a picture of a brighter future and help us believe that we can achieve the things we want to achieve.
3. **They give us a belief in the values that are important to us.**	In doing so, they make us feel part of a team of people that share these values and have the same aims.
4. **They are able to make us feel powerful.**	They allow us the freedom to make decisions about our life, work and the future, especially as a group. They give the group a feeling of power to achieve group goals – the group often becomes a team under an effective leader.

Do these sound like some of the things your personal leaders have done for you? It's more than likely those people who have had a major influence on you, all did these leadership "things" and by definition therefore, can be considered leaders.

These things that all leaders do, are described as the ***conditions that must exist if others are to follow the leader.*** The aim of this book is to help you personally develop these conditions in your own role so that your people will be inclined to follow you as a leader.

5. You may be thinking, "Well, how can I become a leader?"

Why should people do things for you because of who you are not what you are?

When you do become a leader, it is because it is very obvious to others that you are able to establish the conditions that encourage people to follow you. In short, these four conditions detailed above that leaders create, can be described as …

- A shared understanding of the environment - *"We know what we face"*
- A shared vision of where we are going - *"We know what we have to do"*
- A shared set of organisational values - *"We are in this together"*
- A shared feeling of power – *"We can do this"*

Over the next few pages, there's an outline for implementing these four leadership conditions in your role. To help make this section mean something for you personally and for your development as a leader, please now:

- Think about your own situation. Who are your people? What are the challenges facing them?
- Try to imagine how you might start developing these four conditions with your people, your followers.

As you think about your situation, please go back and read these four conditions again. Take particular note of the word *shared". It appears in all four conditions.

6. Why would managers as leaders need to create a *shared understanding of the environment*?

People often work best together and pull together as a team, when they are faced with some kind of external threat that is common to everyone in the team. You may have experienced this yourself at some stage. For instance, this often happens in cases of takeovers and mergers where people who might previously have been a loose working group (sometimes with not a lot in common) are suddenly faced with an external threat that they can't quite understand or manage. Often in these situations, they focus on the things they can manage and the things they do have in common. The external "they" or "them" becomes the common enemy that they can all relate to – they rally around one another to fight this common enemy. Something out there in the environment has come to be seen as a common threat and so, they bond successfully together as a team to fight the common enemy.

But people can also pull together and become very effective as a team when they have a common positive external pressure.

The case of the Training Manager

The Training Manager was working in a financial services organisation when the Marketing Department decided to introduce an incentive scheme. The scheme was designed to encourage each retail branch to reach specific targets. The scheme seemed fair and well thought out. Those branches that exceeded their targets by the largest percentage margins, were to get a considerable reward to be shared among the branch staff.

Now, this type of incentive was new to the organisation. In the Training Manager's opinion, it would be quite contrary to the organisational culture which was very much egalitarian and team based. In addition, the people were already extremely dedicated, loyal and really focused on working together to make the organisation a success.

The Training Manager went to the Marketing Director and told him that he did not think the incentive scheme would work. In fact, he said it could probably be counter productive as it ran contrary to the organisation's culture (the Marketing Director was reasonably new to the organisation). The two of them had numerous long discussions, but in the end, the Marketing Director decided to go with the scheme.

The Training Manager was so confident that he was right, that he told the Marketing Director that he would now, before the scheme started, write the name of the winning branch in a sealed envelope. The Marketing Director could keep and open this envelope only after the incentive scheme was finished.

The scheme was duly conducted and concluded with the winning branch (one of the smaller branches) being named and presented with their award. After the festivities, the Training Manager went to the Marketing

Director and asked him to open the envelope. Out of 127 branches, the Training Manager had correctly selected the winning branch! Needless to say, the Marketing Director was amazed and speechless (well, almost). How did he do it? Was there anything special about the winning branch, e.g. biggest or best territory? No. Was the Training Manager perhaps a clairvoyant? Hardly. Then how was it done?

Prior to the scheme, as soon as the rumor got around that there was to be an incentive scheme for branches, the Training Manager received a phone call from the supervisor of the branch which ultimately won. The supervisor told the Training Manager that her branch would win the contest. It seems that this particular branch, because of its remote location, was rarely visited by people from head office. One of the values shared by people throughout this organisation was that the organisation was seen as a "people place" where people were truly important and so, not to be regularly recognised by the people from head office was seen as a bit of a snub. The supervisor said "We'll win this contest. We'll make them sit up and take notice. I bet we get a lot of visits after this." With that sort of motivation, how could the Training Manager not select them as the winning branch?

In this case, something out there in the environment had come to be seen by the staff of this branch, rather than as a threat, as a common opportunity. So, they bonded even more successfully together as a team to win the contest.

Now does this mean as a new manager, that you have to find some "external enemies" and "external challenges" to be the leader of a successful team? Obviously not. But you can readily see how important it is to make everyone aware of what is happening in the environment and how it might affect them and the team.

How Ann-Mary created a shared understanding of the environment

Ann-Mary was a new Quality Manager in a pharmaceutical manufacturing plant. For the previous four years, the plant had in fact been an R & D facility. Now the product was being launched and was to be manufactured at the same site using the same people. For those of you who have not worked in production or R & D, it's important to know that the type of people attracted to each are quite different. Production type people need to be highly organised, logical, task oriented and be prepared to do the same thing the same way over and over again. Consistency, precision and "getting it right every time" are important to production people. R & D type people on the other hand, need to be creative, analytical and also like to constantly try new ways of doing things.

In addition to re-skilling and re-tasking, Ann-Mary's people needed to fully understand the new environment in which they were now working. Merely retraining them as "production people" would not be enough.

*Some of the things she did as a leader to help her people develop a shared understanding of the **new environment** included:*

- *Business awareness training to help people identify and understand the cost of manufacture, marketing, staffing, pricing, profit margins and so on. Prior to her arrival, millions of dollars had been spent on the facility and the development of the new product over the last four years with no return thus far to the organisation.*
- *Visits by manufacturing people from other parts of the organisation to talk with their counterparts in her facility.*
- *Short exchange programs of key personnel (e.g. supervisors and key technicians) with personnel from other manufacturing sites within the organisation.*
- *Visits by as many staff as possible to other manufacturing organisations.*
- *Visits by representatives of key customer groups to the facility to explain to the staff what they expected as customers.*

Finally, one of the key projects that she introduced and in which key personnel were involved, was to reduce the lead time of manufacture (lead time is the time it takes from start of manufacture to final release of product). This project really helped all personnel focus on the key attributes needed to get product to market in a way that met the financial and quality standards. By working on and completing the project, it gave her people a real understanding of just what production type work is all about.

Ann-Mary's people could then say "We know what we face"

So, that's the first of the four conditions that each leader must establish. Now on to "vision". As you read this section, keep in mind the eight year old who said "Leaders do things first".

7. Why do managers as leaders need to create a *shared vision of where we are going*?

We know from the sports psychologists, that having a vision and specific goals to achieve that vision, are tremendously motivating. If you've been part of a very successful sports team, then there's a very good chance that your team had:

- A vision of where it was going
- Both some short and long term goals to achieve in order to reach that vision

Note: The terms "vision", "mission" and "direction" are used interchangeably here. Many writers have distinguished between the three. However, as a new manager, it's easier for the moment to give the same meaning to all three.

Tim's Case: Creating a shared vision of where the organisation is headed

When Tim, the new CEO took over (even CEO's can be "new managers"), it was a period of rapid growth for both the industry and the organisation. The three main competitors in the market place were known to be best at:

- *Org. A – marketing*
- *Org. B – systems*
- *Org. C – products*

Realising that he had to galvanise the organisation and all the people around a clear direction, Tim looked at both the strengths and limitations of his new organisation. At the same time he had to position the organisation very clearly against the opposition.

At Tim's first major address to the staff and subsequently every time he met formerly with managers and staff, he repeated his "direction" for the organisation. Also, when he talked informally with everyone in the organisation, he was very quick to give examples of the direction the organisation was heading.

At his first formal presentations, he said:

"I believe we are the best provider of customer service in the industry. We have undertaken extensive research, including our Mystery Shopper scheme that you are all aware of. This research consistently places us at No.1 for customer service in our industry. My own observations and informal feedback I have received from customers, confirms what a great job everyone does in providing the best service. We need to maintain our No.1 standing.

"There are at least three other areas of performance by which we can measure ourselves – marketing, systems and products.

"One of our competitors, Organisation A has long been seen as the best marketer in the industry. However, they spend a lot of money to achieve this ranking. We do not intend to spend that amount of money to match them. However, we do need to improve our marketing efforts which could see us move from No.3 to No.2 within the next 9-12 months. Our marketing department is working hard on new programs now and will be asking for your help and support to develop the new programs.

"We can't formally measure ourselves against the competition in terms of systems. We do know however, that some of the others are further advanced than we are, particularly with branch automation. For instance, many of you will have heard that Organisation B has a very good branch system. We will be working hard over the next 12 months to implement the new systems that are now being developed and we will be asking many of you to help in testing and trialing these systems.

"As far as products go, we have products that are comparable with others in the industry, perhaps with the exception of Organisation C. However, we want to be seen as the most innovative in the industry. Over the next 18 months, you will see a number of new products that have never been seen in our industry. I am sure that within this time, we will be seen as No.1 for product innovation"

Tim's address and continued emphasis on his direction for the organisation was motivational. It also resulted in a tremendous shared focus for the organisation. Everyone knew where the organisation was headed. Everyone was clear that they could play a part in achieving the goals that had been set.

As a new manager, what do you need to do, to develop this shared direction for your team? At the end of this chapter, there are guidelines for doing just that. In the meantime, you might start to think about what your team direction should look like.

Here are some thought provoking questions to get you started:

Some key questions for you . . .	Please jot down your thoughts . . .
1. What are the current environmental issues facing my team?	
2. How would my people describe our team to others? e.g. What might they tell their friends about our team?	
3. How would my people describe our team if it were performing at its best?	
4. Would any of the answers be different to those I got from the previous question?	
5. If I was NOT the team's manager, for example, perhaps a manager from another department, how would I judge my team's success?	
6. By the end of the next 12 months, how would I like our team members and others outside the team, to describe my team?	

Once you have answered these questions and developed a direction for your team, your people will be able to say "We now know where we are going".

8. Why do managers as leaders need to create *a shared set of organisational values*?

In my consulting work with hundreds of organisations, I often interview people and run focus groups around management development issues. Three of the questions I always use in these sessions are:

- Why did you join the organisation?
- Why do you stay?
- Why would you leave?

As part of this work, three consistent themes emerge:

1. People join organisations **because of the job**. "The job sounds interesting, challenging and is likely to meet my career aspirations."
2. People stay in the organisation, not only because they like the job, but most importantly because they are working with a group of **like-minded people.** "I enjoy working here. People seem to have a lot in common."
3. People leave an organisation because of **poor management and leadership**. Note: When people actually do leave, they will often give their reasons as "for more money", or "for career progression" – both of which are legitimate. However if you ask these people before they have made up their mind to leave (as an outsider to the organisation, I often have this opportunity), they invariably say "because I am disappointed with the way I am being managed".

People do not leave organisations. They leave bosses!

Now, these are three very important messages for organisations and for you as a new manager. The first one, "the Job" is covered in the chapter on "How to Motivate Others". The third, "Management and Leadership" are continuing themes throughout the book and we have plenty of tips and guidelines on these. Hopefully you've already picked up a few.

It is the second item, "Like-minded People" that we need to turn our minds to now. This will really help you understand why a shared set of organisational values is so important for your development as a leader.

Bob's Case: Creating a shared set of organisational values

I once took up an appointment as Senior Manager Policy and Planning in a medium sized regional bank. My role was to set the HR (people) policies for the organisation. As a new manager to the organisation, I had to quickly come to grips with:

- *What is the current culture of the organisation, particularly in terms of its people management policies, procedures and management style?*
- *What are the challenges facing the organisation at the moment and where is it headed?*
- *How does the culture need to change in order for the organisation to successfully meet these challenges?*

I also had the opportunity to set up a new team of project managers to help develop the necessary HR policies. In doing so, I faced a number of challenges:

- *I was new to the organisation, so it would take some time to under-stand the current culture. I had been told that the current culture was well entrenched but totally outmoded to be able to help it meet the challenges of a changing external environment.*
- *Part of my brief was to help change this culture to help it become more dynamic.*
- *I had to select four project managers who were all capable of de-veloping policy. However, they also had to know how to manage and lead change. Additionally, if they came from within the organi-sation, they could not be embedded in or wedded to, the current cul-ture. If they were external candidates, they must know how to develop an understanding of the culture very quickly.*
- *I had to meld the project managers into a coherent team within a very short space of time so that they could all "sing from the same book" if the culture change was to happen successfully.*

In selecting my project managers, I realised that in addition to having good project management skills, they would need something extra. For me, the most important selection criterion was an "ability to adhere to a

common vision by sharing the same sorts of values."
the people I selected appeared quite different. One was
reer banker; one had been with the company about two
stration. The other two were external appointments
background in marketing and the other in government community ser-
vices.

How did I ensure this new group of people who appeared quite differ-
ent, were in fact like-minded? I started by asking them as part of the se-
lection process, to describe their "ideal organisation". When people
undertake an activity such as this, they always base their answers on
their own beliefs about what a perfect organisation should look like. It
was then a simple matter to look for people whose values matched mine
and each other's. (At the end of this chapter I have some guidelines in-
cluding an exercise called "The Ideal Organisation" that will help you
understand the values your current team members hold. If you wish, you
may also adapt the "Ideal Organisation" exercise for recruiting new
people.)

Was my "shared values" strategy successful?

One measure of success would of course be the successful implementation of policies to assist the culture change process. And this did occur.
However, there's another measure of success of "like-mindedness". Our
team of five, who are now all in different roles and different organisations, still maintain contact and get together from time to time fifteen
years after our project work has finished! At these get-togethers we often tell stories and talk about how "We were in that together". In fact,
as I write this chapter it is just three weeks to our next reunion, which I
am really looking forward to.

9. Why do managers as leaders need to create *a shared feeling of power*?

The fourth element of leadership, "power", is often confused with the
power of the leader and can sometimes have a negative connotation.
That's because we tend to relate power with people who seem to be using their power in a negative way. As an element of leadership however,
this aspect of power is not about personal power or positional power,
but rather:

- The "power" **people feel** when they are able to make their own decisions about their work and the way it is done, without having to refer to an authority figure such as their manager. Some writers refer to this as "empowerment". Others have referred to it as "freedom".
- The "power" a **team feels** when it has achieved something that is over and above what others might have thought possible. This definition of power can often be seen within groups where there is a charismatic leader. For example, after WWII, researchers tried to understand how Hitler could have led the German people so far astray. Interviewers said to those who had attended the mass rallies "you must have felt overwhelmed by his power". They said "No. He made us feel powerful, as though we could achieve anything."

The first of these types of power, **empowering people** by allowing them the freedom to make decisions within their area of responsibility, is one of the essential skills a new manager needs to develop. It has three components:

1. Setting and agreeing **performance standards** with each person for his or her role
2. **Delegating** meaningful tasks and responsibilities to enable people to achieve their goals
3. Providing people with **feedback** on how well they have met the agreed performance expectations

Because empowering your people is such an important part of a new manager's role, all three components – performance standards, delegating, and feedback - will be dealt with in detail in later chapters.

So, your people as individuals, need to feel powerful by having power over how they undertake their role. But they also need to feel powerful as a team. This is our second type of power and one that you will need to develop as a leader.

How Tim created the shared feeling of power within his team

Remember Tim, the CEO of the financial services company mentioned earlier. He showed how a shared feeling of power can be achieved by trusting people. As part of his drive for new products, his Product De-

velopment team designed a product that was completely different to any-thing yet seen in the industry. The development of the new product in-volved major system changes, new product marketing and in some cases physical reconstruction of the 127 branches, and of course, intensive staff training.

At the outset of the product development period, all 600 staff throughout HO and the 127 branches, were briefed on the new product. They were told the part they would play in it and that it would take six months to get the product to market. They were also told that it must remain secret if the organisation were to take a march on the competition.

Some six months later, one Friday afternoon, Tim held a press confer-ence to announce the new product. It would be available when the or-ganisation opened its doors for business on Monday morning. The product marketing was launched that evening and continued over the weekend with major press saturation.

The launch of this new product quickly gained Tim's organisation in-creased market share. The industry was amazed and everyone within Tim's organisation was abuzz with what they had achieved. Can you imagine how powerful Tim's 600 people felt that Friday evening and the following Monday when the product was launched? The incredible thing about this case, is that over the six months of product development, 600 people were able to keep it secret – not one word got out to the industry!

The shared feeling of "We can do this" was obviously in place through-out that six months in Tim's organisation.

Hopefully, the explanation of the four conditions that leaders create, namely ...

- A shared understanding of the environment - "We know what we face"
- A shared vision of where we are going - "We know what we have to do"
- A shared set of organisational values - "We are in this together"
- A shared feeling of power – "We can do this"

31

has commenced your thinking about how you might start developing these four conditions in your own workplace with your people.

HOW TO IMPLEMENT THE IDEAS IN THIS CHAPTER

 How to start *Leading* straight away

Display leadership . . .	Actions to take . . .
1. Help your people understand and make sense of **their environment**	• Talk with your people regularly about the strengths and weaknesses of the organisation and your team and how you, with their help, will manage these. • Discuss regularly the opportunities and threats facing the team and the organisation and how you can make the most of these.
2. Give your people a **sense of direction**	• Spend 80% of your communication time and content talking about the future. • Show your people how they and your team fit into the bigger organisational picture.
3. Help your people develop a **sense of team** by having a belief in the **values** that are important to them	• Talk regularly about your own values and why they are important to you. • Discuss with people why they work here – encourage and reinforce these at every opportunity.
4. Help make your people **feel powerful**	• Allow people the opportunity to take responsibility, make decisions and take risks. • Talk positively and frequently about team wins.

 How to fully implement *Leading*, get your followers on board and totally committed

Remember, Leading is all about establishing the conditions that will encourage others to follow you by developing a **shared**:

- understanding of the **environment**,
- understanding of the **direction** your team is taking,
- set of **team values**,
- feeling of **power**.

This will take you some time, so be patient,

- plan the following exercises over the coming three to six months
- at the end of the explanation of these exercises, you will find a time table template that will be ideal for planning their implementation

PHASE 1: How to develop a shared understanding of the environment

This has three parts. Firstly, find out the issues facing the organisation. Secondly, establish the issues and challenges facing your team. Finally, communicate, communicate, communicate these within your team.

1. Find out what are the issues, concerns challenges and problems facing your **organisation**		
Step 1:	Involve your boss and key stakeholders	• Talk with your manager and other key people in the organisation. Draw up a list of the critical issues they see that are facing the organisation. • You could also send out a short survey and then discuss the results with key people.
Step 2:	Place the critical issues in order of priority	• As you develop your list, ask people to prioritise them in terms of their importance to the organisation's success.
Step 3:	Agree your findings with your manager	• Before communicating and discussing these with your team, have a final discussion with your manager to agree the importance ranking for the issues you have identified.

2. Find out what are the issues, concerns challenges and problems facing your **people**		
Step 1:	Plan to talk individually with each team member	• Let your people know that you will have individual sessions with each to discuss the key issues and challenges for them.

Step 2:	**Ask team members for their issues**	• Ask them to draw up a list of the issues they would like to discuss. Explain why you are doing this. Talk with each of your people individually. Ask them to prioritize the issues.
Step 3:	**Address the minor issues first and explain why**	• Before your next team meeting, try to address as many of the minor issues as possible. Make a diary note to start work on the more important issues.

3. Communicate on a regular basis what is happening in the environment that will or may affect your team		
Step 1:	**Discuss the critical organisation issues**	• At your next team meeting and every subsequent meeting, discuss the key issues that were prioritized by management.
Step 2:	**Ask team members to address the critical organisation issues**	• Ask for input on how the team might start addressing or assisting the organisation to meet some of these challenges.
Step 3:	**Show how minor team issues have already been addressed**	• Mention the team-related issues that you identified and have already addressed.
Step 4:	**Ask the team for their help to work on the remaining team issues**	• Discuss those team issues that are yet to be addressed and get the team's help to address them.

Phases 2 & 3: These can be completed in tandem:

- **How to develop a shared understanding of the <u>direction</u> your team needs to take, and**
- **How to develop a shared set of <u>team values</u>**

Step 1: Review the main environmental issues from your earlier environmental analysis and discussions	• What are the three or four key challenges facing your team (organisational, team and individual)? • List these out very clearly in dot point form – if possible, one short sentence for each. • Put this list aside until you have conducted the "Ideal Organisation" exercise listed in the next step. • As part of the "Ideal Organisation" exer-

	cise you are about to undertake, you will be able to clarify and define a direction for your team as well as defining the team member's shared values.
Step 2: Get your team together for an "Ideal Organisation" session. This is best done over two to three hours and is ideal for an off-site get together	Ask each team member to answer the following without discussing it with their team mates: • What drives you to succeed at work? List as many things as you can think of. • What are the aspects about your work or place of work that you value? If you wish, you could issue these questions as pre-work for the team session.
Step 3: At the "Ideal Organisation" team session, run a group discussion to uncover shared values using these three prompts . . .	1. Describe the type of organisation you would ideally like to work in, i.e. your "ideal organisation" 2. Why would this be your ideal?" (The answers to this "Why?" question are in fact their values.) 3. List these as dot points for everyone to see, discuss and agree as shared values.
Step 4: Identify both the "facilitators" and "inhibitors" to achieving the ideal organisation	Ask the team to discuss and list: • What are the things that are currently helping to make our team similar to our ideal organisation? • What are the things that are currently hindering or preventing our team from being more like our ideal?
Step 5: Complete your Team Direction statement – you can do this as part of the "Ideal Organisation" session or afterwards by yourself, then communicate about it regularly with your team	• Revisit the list of key challenges you developed in Step 1. Add to, or amend these based on the Ideal Organisation team session. • Write these out as goals to be achieved, i.e. What does the team need to do to meet the challenges and move toward becoming an ideal team? • For each goal, describe the shared team values that will help the team reach the desired goal.

Phase 4: How to develop a shared feeling of power

The following points are not sequential. You should undertake them as often as possible.	
Communicate the team direction	• Talk regularly with the team and individual members, about the goals to be achieved. • Look for and praise team members whenever you see behaviour that reinforces one of the team values.
Talk positively and frequently about team wins	• Celebrate when the team does something well or achieves a good result. • Have small get-togethers over tea, coffee or drinks, or for really big wins, take them off site for a get-together. • Acknowledge setbacks but focus on how the team will now move forward.
Run frequent team sessions similar to the "Ideal Organisation"	• Get your team together whenever there is a major issue or challenge. Ask for their input on how the challenge might best be met. (there are two chapters later in the book on how to run such meetings)
Allow people the freedom to make decisions within their area of responsibility	• Encourage people to take initiative. • Recognise and praise those team members who are prepared to "have a go".

✓ **Your plan of action – activities, dates, people to involve**

Developing leadership takes time.

However, if you take it in small steps, a little at a time, you'll soon be amazed at the progress. Whenever I am faced with a task that seems very large and I start to procrastinate about starting, I think of that old Chinese saying that "a journey of a thousand miles starts with the first step". Just make sure that you do take that first step. It is so easy to find reasons to put it off 'till tomorrow.

To assist with your planning and implementation, following is a template where you can put dates and follow your progress. The process described earlier in the chapter has been simplified so that there are only five main items you need to carry out over the next 3 to 6 months.

It is suggested that you complete this plan as soon as possible and share it with the key people in your role – your manager and your team – and get started. That way you will be committed.

Plan for putting "leadership" into action

Item	Date to implement	Action to take	People to involve	Follow-up date	Follow-up action
1.		Talk with your boss and others to ascertain critical issues facing the organisation.	• Boss • Key stake-holders		• Develop list of critical issues • Rank these by importance • Discuss and agree ranking with your manager
2.		Hold an individual discussion with each team member to ascertain the concerns, issues or problems they face.	• Each team member		• Develop a list of common items • Address individual items • Address minor team items
3.		At next team meeting, outline: • the key issues identified by management • the common team issues • ask for their input to work on those items that are within their control to change	• Team		• Draw up an action plan with responsibilities for various team members and follow up dates
4.		Run an "Ideal Organisation" team meeting (preferably off site).	• Team		• Draw up a list of the team values • Develop a vision of where the team is headed
5		"Walk the Talk" – make sure that you now: • Discuss the team direction with others at every opportunity • Do what you said you would do with each of the action items	• Team • Direct manager • Other key stakeholders		• Follow up to ensure that all agreed actions by yourself and various team members are being implemented • Hold a follow-up meeting three months later to discuss progress

Remember to read Chapter Two on the other two elements of a manager's role - Managing and Operating - before getting too far into the above activity.

Chapter 2

What does it take to be an Effective Manager?

1. You as a *Manager* – the second element of the Manager's Role

In Chapter One, we looked at you as a Leader. The second element of your role, the "Manager" part, is the formal part of your role – the part that is described in your role or position description and the one that you will be held accountable for by the organisation. It includes two aspects:

- getting things done, i.e. the tasks that must be achieved
- through people, i.e. the people that must be managed and developed

As we saw in Chapter One, the Leading element of your role is very much future oriented and about setting direction, building shared values and developing team power. The Managing element on the other hand, is more about the day-to-day tasks of managing. Theodore Levitt (1925-2006) is said to have once described these role elements as:

- Leading is path **finding** and
- Managing is path **minding**

Managing is mandatory, leading is optional.

A famous study after WWII sheds some light on this distinction. During WWII, Ohio State University in the US was asked by the US government to look at selection processes for deciding amongst the thousands of troops being drafted for the war, who would be best suited to attend officer training. Their research confirmed the earlier writings of Mary Parker Follett (remember, she was the person who almost 100 years ago described a manager's role as "getting things done through people") that there were two components to effective management:

- a **Task** focus (the getting things done part)
- a **Relationship** focus (the through people part)

Building on the Ohio study, other researchers found that some managers in their day-to-day activities may focus directly on the task, others may focus on relationships with the people, while others may try various blends of task and relationship focus. What will work well for one manager in one situation may not work well for another manager in other situations. It has also been found that the task and relationship focus a manager emphasizes in his or her formal role, is independent of his or her status as a leader.

What are some of these "task" and "relationship" type activities that make up the managing element of your manager's role? Here's a list that was drawn up by my colleague, Dennis Pratt. See if you can recognise some of the things you do in your day-to-day role as a manager. As you read through the list, you may also get an idea of whether you tend to be more task focused, relationship focused or a combination of both task and relationship focused in your role.

The following are managerial "task" type activities ...	The following are managerial "relationship" type activities ...
• Designing the team's overall structure. i.e. how the various jobs in the team are designed and put together to work best • Ensuring that every job within the team is well-defined and can be linked with all the other jobs into an effective team. • Selecting team members for roles within the team - making sure that 'the right person is in the right job'. • Clearly defining and communicating specific team objectives. • Discussing and agreeing individual job requirements, accountabilities and responsibilities with team members.	• Personally helping to link the team and its individual members together into an effective whole. • Delegating appropriate decision-making authority to members of the team and holding them accountable for results. • Providing feedback to team members on team and individual performance. • Providing opportunities for team members to develop their own skills and careers. • Coaching team members to improve job skills and knowledge

In terms of the degree of task and relationship required in your role . . .

- Do you tend to be more "task" or "relationship" focused in your role, or perhaps a bit of both?
- Is this appropriate for you in your situation? e.g. is it a role that requires a lot of task focus? or relationship focus? or both?
- Should you do more or less of any of these to increase your effectiveness?

2. You as an *Operator* – the third element of the Manager's Role

In addition to Leading and Managing, is there anything more to being an effective manager?

To help answer this, here are two interesting questions for you:

1. Why did you get promoted or selected for your role as a manager?
2. Did your employers know about your management and leadership skills before they selected you for the role?

It would probably be fair to say that you got promoted because you were extremely good at your old job of technical or professional expert. However, your employer probably had very few clues about your prowess as a manager of people.

In your previous position, you acted in the role of operator, or technician or professional, producing your own outputs or results. You were expected to accept accountability for your own work - producing the required quantity of output, and maintaining the quality or accuracy of your results. Obviously you did very well to be recognised and promoted as a potential manager by your employer.

Now as you take up your formal position as a manager, you are expected to accept accountability for more than just your own work. You will also be held accountable for the work of a team of people. But there will still be a part of your managerial role that only you can do – this part of your manager's role is called "operating".

Operating involves performing operator/technician functions that do not fall within the elements of either leading or managing. For example, managing was defined as 'getting things done through other people', but there are times when the manager has to 'get things done' himself or herself.

The reason why these things cannot be delegated to others may include role definition – e.g. it is the manager's job to do the budgets. It may include expertise - nobody else in the team knows how to do this. It may include time or staff numbers available - there is nobody else who can do this at the moment.

There will be greater individual differences among managers in operator / technician behaviours than in either of the other two elements of the manager's role. For example, a manager in charge of a large team may do very little operating. On the other hand, a leading hand or supervisor with one other person in the team may do very little else.

Here (once again thanks to Dennis Pratt) are some examples of things that make up the operator element of the manager's role:

The following are managerial "operator" type activities ...
• Drawing up plans and budgets.
• Writing reports on team performance or operational issues.
• Preparing professional / technical reports or recommendations for other parts of the organisation.
• Contributing technical expertise at meetings or to projects.
• Completing assigned project tasks.
• Negotiating contracts.
• Making technical decisions within your own area of expertise.
• Answering questions and giving advice to other members of the team.
• Doing much the same work (perhaps at a higher level) as other members of the team.
• Keeping up to date technically, and involving yourself in skills and career development activities.

To summarise what was discussed in Chapter One and what we have covered so far in this chapter, there are three distinctly different elements in your formal role of manager:

- **Leading;** giving a positive direction to the whole team and to people in the team by establishing the four conditions that will encourage the people to follow you,
- **Managing;** getting the things done that need to be done through all the other people in the team, and
- **Operating;** getting some of those things done yourself, just like any other operator or technician.

A shorthand way of remembering these three role elements is that:

- <u>**Leading**</u> **is "Path finding"** – setting the direction and engaging the team to follow
- <u>**Managing**</u> **is "Path minding"** – having set the direction, ensuring that everyone is meeting the standards and that people are being trained and developed to achieve at their best
- <u>**Operating**</u> **is "Doing"** – performing operator/technical/professional tasks that do not fall within leading and managing

One of the tricks to becoming an effective manager, is to limit the amount of operating you do, so that you can focus on the other parts of your role – leading and managing. It's your ability and willingness to focus on the leading and managing elements that will provide you with the biggest payouts as a manager.

3. How much Leading, Managing and Operating should you do? Is there an ideal mix of Leading, Managing, Operating?

That's a question that is often asked by new managers. The short answer? There is no "ideal". Each managerial role will be different depending on the emphasis that is needed in the three role elements in order to be successful. Over time however, it is preferable that you should try to:

- place more emphasis on the leading element
- maintain the focus on the managing element

- lessen the physical amount of time you spend focusing on the operating element.

The following diagram shows how the emphasis on the three role elements may change as you progress through various levels of management during your career.

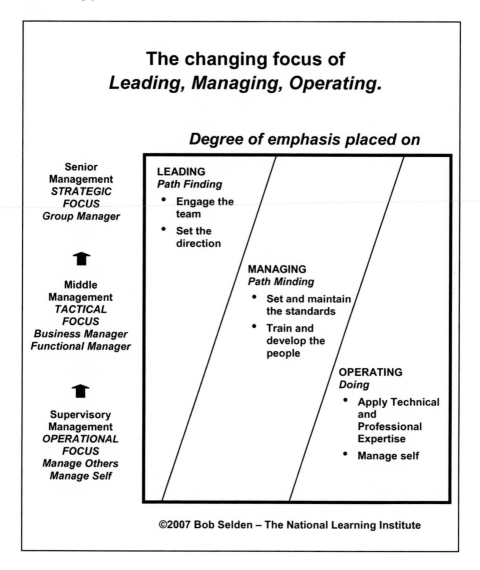

The changing focus of
Leading, Managing, Operating.

Degree of emphasis placed on

Senior Management
STRATEGIC FOCUS
Group Manager

LEADING
Path Finding
- Engage the team
- Set the direction

Middle Management
TACTICAL FOCUS
Business Manager
Functional Manager

MANAGING
Path Minding
- Set and maintain the standards
- Train and develop the people

Supervisory Management
OPERATIONAL FOCUS
Manage Others
Manage Self

OPERATING
Doing
- Apply Technical and Professional Expertise
- Manage self

©2007 Bob Selden – The National Learning Institute

Getting the balance "right" between the three role elements will be one of the challenges for you as a new manager. The following activities will help you make the most appropriate balance choice.

HOW TO IMPLEMENT THE IDEAS IN THIS CHAPTER

⚑ **How to improve your role as Leader, Manager and Operator straight away**

Leading, Managing, Operating (LMO)	Actions to take . . .
• What do you do that is Leading, Managing, Operating?	• Look back over a typical day. What do you do that is Leading, Managing, Operating? • On a percentage basis, how much of your time is focused on Leading? Managing? Operating?
• How much Leading, Managing, Operating should you be doing?	• Give a percentage to where you should be placing your emphasis on LMO. • From the list of LMO activities at the end of this chapter, select three that you could do more of or less of, to move your percentage closer to where you think it should be.

⚑ **How to get the best balance of Leading, Managing, Operating for you as a new manager**

For those who prefer the Reflective and Theorist style of learning, you will like the following activity. Activists will see the benefit. Pragmatists will probably find it painful! However, whatever your learning style, this is one of the most important learning activities you will ever undertake as a manager. It will require you to identify how much of your time is currently spent on leading, managing, operating and then assess how appropriate this split is to your effectiveness in your role.

Step 1: Log your work activities for one week

Keep a log of your activities for one week. At the end of the week, go back through your log and Identify each activity as leading, managing or operating -included at the end of this activity is a list of typical activities that fall under each element. A simple way of doing this is to split your day into half-hour segments on a sheet of paper and mark each major activity during that half-hour as leading, managing or operating. At the end of the week, add up the number of half-hours you have spent on each role element and give them a percentage:

1. Approximately how much of your working time (expressed as a percentage) do you currently spend in "Leading" behaviour?

%

2. Approximately how much of your working time (expressed as a percentage) do you currently spend in "Managing" behaviour?

%

3. Approximately how much of your working time (expressed as a percentage) do you currently spend in "Operating" behaviour?

%

Step 2: Decide the appropriateness of your current balance of Leading, Managing, Operating

Is this percentage appropriate for your current effectiveness? What would be a more appropriate balance of the three elements in your current role?

Leading . . .

%

Managing . . .

%

Operating . . .

%

Step 3: Decide what you need to change and the implications of these changes

If you decided that you need to change the balance of LMO in your current role

1. What can you do more of ... ? (Identify some behaviours)

2. ... so that you can do less of ... ? (identify some behaviours)

3. What are the implications for you if you make these changes?

4. How will you manage these implications?

Step 4: Repeat the time log to check progress

Repeat the time log in six months time to see how your plan has developed.

 Your plan of action – activities, dates, people to involve

Step	Date to implement	Action to ake	People to involve	Follow-up date	Follow-up action
1.		• Keep a one week log of your activities. • Break each day down into half hour segments. • Use the list of activities at the end of this chapter to identify all your activities as either L, M, or O.	• Self		• Decide how much of your time as a % you currently focus on Leading, Managing, Operating?
2.		Is the % split of Leading, Managing, Operating appropriate for you in your role?	• Self • Your manager if this is appropriate		• If the % split is ok, you are off to a flying start. If not, • What should the % split be?
3.		Decide which actions you can: • do more of, • do less of, to improve your LMO balance.	• Self • Your manager if this is appropriate		• Implement the LMO actions you have decided upon immediately.
4.		Re-do the time log in six months time.	• Self • Your manager if this is appropriate		• Make any necessary changes.

Some examples of activities that make up the three role elements

Leading type activities	Managing type activities	Operating type activities
• Conveying a vision of what the future should look like.	• Designing the team's overall structure. i.e. how the various jobs in the team are designed and put together to work best	• Drawing up plans and budgets.
• Using positive language that describes ideal outcomes.	• Ensuring that every job within the team is well-defined and can be linked with all the other jobs into an effective team.	• Writing reports on team performance or operational issues.
• Setting high standards of performance for the team.		• Preparing professional / technical reports or recommendations for other parts of the organisation.
• Acting as an example for team members to follow that is consistent with what you say you should do.	• Selecting team members for roles within the team - making sure that 'the right person is in the right job'.	• Contributing technical expertise at meetings or to projects.
• Accepting ownership and responsibility for your own decisions and accountability for team problems.	• Clearly defining and communicating specific team objectives.	• Completing assigned project tasks.
	• Personally helping to link the team and its individual members together into an effective whole.	• Negotiating contracts.
• Clarifying and communicating any issues 'from above' or from other parts of the organisation that may affect the team.		• Making technical decisions within his/her own area of expertise.
	• Discussing and agreeing individual job requirements, accountabilities and responsibilities with team members.	• Answering questions and giving advice to other members of the team.
• Promoting your team and representing your team's view-point, needs and concerns to others in the organisation.	• Delegating appropriate decision-making authority to members of the team and holding them accountable for results.	• Doing much the same work (perhaps at a higher level) as other members of the team.
• Helping and encouraging the team to recognise and act on opportunities that may improve their success.	• Providing feedback to team members on team and individual performance.	• Keeping up to date technically, and involving yourself in skills and career development activities
• Helping the team deal effectively with threats to their successful performance or operations.	• Providing opportunities for team members to develop their own skills and careers.	
• Assisting the team to overcome disappointments.	• Coaching team members to improve job skills and knowledge	
• Creating an environment where team members feel their strengths are being recognised and their weaknesses are being compensated for.		

• Conducting future oriented, problem solving meetings that will improve ways of operating or team working.	• Conducting information sharing meetings. • Attending meetings on behalf of the team.	• Participating in technical / professional and / or operational / administration type meetings.

Part 2: Managing Your Team

They've given you a team. Now what do you do?

Part 2 sets out the eight key elements to successfully develop and lead your team. It starts with "Team Work" and then follows a logical sequence from "Selection" through to "Managing Appraisals". However, in practise, on the job, you will find yourself using these at various times. "Feedback" for instance, should be used constantly. It also includes a chapter on "How to fire someone" (if you really have to).

Learning tips to help you get the most out of Part 2 . . .

Activists:

- Go straight to Chapter 6 "How to motivate others" – it has the most immediate benefits for you. Complete the activity at the end of the chapter.
- Have lunch with a colleague and ask their

views on how they motivate others.

- Test yourself on the checklist, "The Team Leader's Health Check-Up" at the end of Chapter 3.
- Go to the other chapters when you have a real need, although it is suggested that Chapter 5 "How to set performance standards" is a must read.

Pragmatists:

- Go straight to Chapter 9 "How to manage the appraisal process". Implement the quarterly review process described there, immediately.
- Go to the other chapters when you have a real need.
- The exercise at the end of Chapter 3, "The Team Leader's Health Check-Up" could also be useful for you.

Theorists

- Go straight to Chapter 8 "Coaching – how to help your people take commitment for their own development". This has all the feeling type stuff.
- Then start at Chapter 3 and read the remaining chapters in sequence.

Reflectors:

- Start with Chapter 3, then read the others in sequence.
- Diarise to have regular meetings with your colleague on the chapters you find most interesting. Remember to take notes for these meetings (I'm sure you will).

Chapter 3

Team Work

As a new manager, being successful takes more than just individual effort - it takes team work. For team work to be successful, teams and individual team members need to have clearly understood team goals; a sense of commitment to those team goals; the ability to work together; mutual accountability; and all the resources and skills needed to achieve those goals.

There are five process steps to developing and maintaining team work –

1. Decide whether you have or want a team
2. Define your role as team leader
3. Define the current team status
4. Get your team engaged
5. Focus on "process" management as well as "content" management

Step 1: Decide whether you have or want a team

Do you have a team or a group?

Many managers waste a lot of time trying to develop team work amongst a group of people reporting to them who do not have any need to work cooperatively together, or form up as a team. They all have different functions and they don't rely on each other to achieve their individual results.

So, what's the difference between a group and a team?

Groups are formed by at least two people who interact and may share some interrelated task goals. However, the majority of the work group members do can be done without relying on other members of the group. For example, often the "top team" of the organisation is in fact a group rather than a team. The members each have a very defined area of responsibility - perhaps they all contribute to the broad goal of "organisation success" and perhaps there are elements of collaboration required to achieve that broad goal - but most of their own function may be successfully managed without having to rely on all of the other "top team" members.

Teams on the other hand, are groups that have three additional characteristics that set them apart:

- Members must depend on one another to achieve their task goals
- Each member must have a particular role to play in the team
- There must be team goals and objectives that can only be achieved by all the team members contributing to a team total output. (In a team, If one member doesn't fulfill his or her role, it's not just that person's own functional area that fails, the whole team fails.)

As a result of these characteristics, members are required to interact with one another quite differently when they are members of a team as shown in the following diagram.

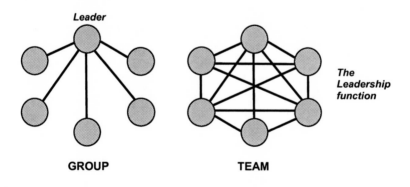

Read through some of the common differences in the table below. As you do, think about your own people – do they form part of a group or are they a team?

Characteristics of Groups ☑	Characteristics of Teams ☑
☐ Individual accountability – members are primarily concerned with achieving their own objectives.	☐ Accountability – whilst individual members have specific objectives, they are primarily concerned with the contribution of those objectives to achieving the team's goals.
☐ Group leadership is generally through positional authority (e.g. the manager, CEO, etc.).	☐ Team leadership may initially be through positional authority (e.g. manager) but at times can also be taken by other members (e.g. project teams) or handed over by the manager for specific tasks (e.g. problem solving meetings).
☐ Groups will sometimes work collaboratively but members put their own objectives foremost.	☐ Members work collaboratively and respect other team members because they need to achieve common goals and objectives.
☐ Often the manager determines and plans the work of his/her group members and the jobs are narrowly defined.	☐ In the team environment the manager collaborates with members as a peer and jointly establishes and plans the work.

Here's a practical example that may help you decide whether your current group of people is, or should be, a team. Picture for a moment the games of cricket and baseball. While they are somewhat different in their rules and the way each game is played (at least they both use a small, round ball), they do share some distinct similarities that require each game to be played by a team, not a group.

For instance in both cricket and baseball:

- Every member has to be able to bat – the team goal is to score more runs than the opposition.
- Every member has to be able to throw and catch a ball – they must all have at least a basic level of hand/eye coordination. The team goal is to restrict the opposition to as few runs as possible.
- Some members, as well as being able to bat, throw and catch, need to have specialist skills if the team is to be successful. In baseball, for example, it's the pitcher and catcher; in cricket it's the bowler and wicket keeper.

- In both games, teams can only be successful when every member of the team feels confident that he or she can rely on every other member of the team to make a competent contribution and do his or her job well.

Does your situation call for team work or group work?

Why is this difference important?

If you think that your people form a team, or you believe your situation calls for team work rather than group work, then as their manager here are some important considerations for you:

Team Characteristic . . .	Questions to answer . . .
• The skills required in a team are broader than a group and provide for individual growth and development.	☐ Do I provide cross training? ☐ Do I encourage members to work directly with other team members?
• Because people have to work together to achieve common goals, their learning is continuous and becomes part of the culture of the team.	☐ How do I help the team establish their common goals? ☐ Is there a team culture and what should I do to promote that culture?
• Because accountability exists for achieving the team's goals, people work together, rather than working individually on specific tasks as happens in groups.	☐ How do I help members decide how they will contribute to the team's goals? ☐ Do team members have "team development" as part of their performance objectives?
• In groups, the rewards are based on individual performance and the manager determines who gets what. In teams, however, rewards are based on both individual performance and the individual's contribution to the team's overall performance.	☐ Have I clearly linked rewards to each member's contribution to team development and team performance? ☐ Are people clearly aware of the rewards for their commitment to the team?
• In groups, there is a very clear and appointed leader. In teams, the leader may be formally appointed (you), but leadership as a process will move around within the group depending on the situation and the team's needs.	☐ As part of my role as a manager, am I also ready to take on the role of team leader? ☐ How will I encourage team members to take a leadership role when there is the need to do so?

You can readily see that deciding that your people should form a team makes your role as their leader very important. It will be critical to the team's success.

However, if you decide that there is no need for your people to become a team (and this can be quite legitimate, depending on your situation), then your role as their manager will be different. You will still need all the people skills required of a team leader, but you may need to apply them differently. For example:

- perhaps there will be more direction given by you rather than consultation or consensus seeking;
- your meetings are likely to be more information sharing rather than problem solving;
- your meetings are also likely to be less frequent as there will be little pressure to meet to solve problems - everyone will have different problems;
- most importantly, you will have a lot more one-to-one communication with members rather than one-to-team or one-within-team communication.

If that's your decision, there's no need to read any further in this chapter. There are many other chapters that will assist with your people management skill development (e.g. motivation, appraisals, meetings and so on).

Step 2: Define your role as team leader

What role model are you setting for your team? What should be the model you are setting? It has often been said that "the team is a reflection of its leader." If you're not clear on the role you want to play as team leader, then your team members will be unsure as well.

Included at the end of this chapter is a "Team Leader's Health Check-Up" to help you check your current status and build your role as team leader.

Step 3: Define the current team status

At what stage is your team now?

Now that you've decided that your people do form a team, it's time to get down to business.

Team work, team work, team work! You can say it "until the cows come home". But saying "team work" and doing "team work" are two completely different things. The challenge in this chapter is to avoid too much "saying" and get straight into the "doing".

The best way to start doing team work is to describe your team to some-one else. Tell your partner or a good friend about your team by answer-ing the following questions (write your answers down on a sheet of paper):

---

1. My team is made up of . . . (your team member's names)

2. The aim of my team is to . . .

3. We do this by . . .

4. The challenges we face are . . .

5. I would rate my team as:

    > ☐ Successful
    > ☐ Somewhat successful
    > ☐ Less than successful

    Because . . .

6. If I had to give my team a name, I would call it "(a one word ad-jective)"

What does your team look like now?

Forcing you to describe your team to someone else, perhaps for the first time, really can help you start to crystallise your actual opinion of your team as its leader. It will give you a personal benchmark from which to move forward (if your team is already performing well, it can help your team develop even further).

Once you have written out the answers to the six questions and shared them with your partner, friend or colleague, you should then share them with your team. Your feedback to your team about how you view the team and their responses, will be critical to growing and developing real team work. (There's an explanation of how to run this meeting at the end of this chapter). The sharing of views through a meeting such as this, enables all people within the team to gain a common understanding of how one another views the team - what it does – their roles - and the challenges the team faces.

So, the third step in developing team work is to define the current look or state of the team. The other two process steps essential for developing your team are:

- Getting the members *ENGAGED*
- Regularly focussing on managing team *PROCESS*

Step 4: Get your team engaged

Now, is your team engaged?

Many supervisors, managers and team leaders bemoan the fact that their team is not totally engaged with or committed to what he or she is trying to achieve. Is it poor communication on the boss's part? Lack of direction? Lack of or little motivation from the team members?

A recent survey by the Corporate Leadership Council reported that from a study of 50,000 employees worldwide, only 11% reported that they felt fully engaged in their current work, 76% felt neither engaged nor disengaged and 13% felt fully disengaged.

Where do your team members stand?

> ☐ Fully engaged?
> ☐ Neither engaged nor disengaged?
> ☐ Disengaged?

Before you answer that, or perhaps before you start putting the names of some of your team members into the three categories (which can be a useful exercise for you as the team's top member), it's worthwhile visiting the dictionary definition of the word "engagement".

Engagement

1. The act of engaging, pledging, enlisting, occupying, or entering into contest.
2. The state of being engaged, pledged or occupied; specifically, a pledge to take some one as husband or wife.
3. That which engages; engrossing occupation; employment of the attention; obligation by pledge, promise, or contract an enterprise embarked in.

Can we gain some ideas about engaging our teams by taking a lead from each of the three definitions – namely, "external contest", "pledge to take on" and "engrossing"?

What happens in practise? Do organisations engage their people by "defining the contest", "getting them to pledge their commitment" and "providing engrossing challenges"?

In their studies of some 300 organisations who were actively working on engagement strategies, the Corporate Leadership Council summarised the strategies of the more successful organisations as:

*   Diagnosing the urgency of the engagement challenge
*   Determining the organisational strategy that engages managers and employees

- Creating engagement opportunities to enable employee contribution
- Framing an engaging structure that builds organisational credibility with employees
- Benchmarking engagement over time for continuous improvement

Following are some tips for building engagement within your team.

4.1 Define the external contest

People often work best together and pull together as a team when they are faced with some kind of external threat that is common to everyone in the team. For instance, this often happens in cases of takeovers and mergers where people who might previously have been a loose working group (sometimes with not a lot in common) are suddenly faced with an external threat that they can't quite understand or manage. Often in these situations, they focus on the things they can manage and the things they do have in common. The external "they" or "them" becomes the common enemy that they can all relate to – they rally around one another to fight this common enemy. Something out there in the environment has come to be seen as a common threat and so, they bond successfully together as a team to fight the common enemy.

But people can also pull together and become very effective as a team when they have a common positive external pressure, such as winning a contest, or being seen as the "best" team. As a team leader, the secret is to identify what in the external environment might be the threats and opportunities the team can bond around.

In Chapter One, we dealt extensively with the need for you as a leader to develop within your team a shared understanding of the environment. If you have already run the "Ideal Organisation" workshop mentioned there with your team, you and your team will now be very much aware of any external contests the team may face.

4.2 Get team members to pledge their commitment

Does this mean getting them to sign a formal document, or have them all stand and sing the company song? In my own culture, probably not (although in other cultures I have heard of organisations doing just that). What it does mean is getting your team members on board by being attuned to their values and motives and aligning these with your team direction. Once again, if you have run the "Ideal Organisation" workshop mentioned previously, you will be aware of team values. If not, it is suggested that you run it now.

4.3 Provide engrossing challenges

It will be extremely difficult to get team member engagement if the work that your team members do is dull and boring. All the studies of motivation over the last 50 years include at least the following to build motivation:

- **Achievement** – people need to see results for what they do. Make sure that their work is able to be measured, preferably by each team member themselves.

- **Recognition for achievement** – praise and recognise team members for the work that they do well. Encourage team members to praise one another. Set the example and build a culture of recognition by finding at least one of your team members doing something well every day and praise them for it.

- **Responsibility** – encourage people to take responsibility for their actions. Allow them to make decisions (without the need to refer to you) within their area of responsibility.

- **Meaningful, interesting work** – ensure the work is meaningful to each individual. Assign people to work that they find satisfying. Look for ways to make the work more interesting – get your team members involved by asking for their ideas on how to make their jobs more interesting.

- **Growth and advancement** – provide team members with the opportunity to develop themselves both personally and professionally. Your aim is to have the most marketable team members in the organisation. You will know when you are successful at this, when your fellow managers keep wanting your people to join their team. When you develop this type of team culture, you'll have people lining up at your door wanting to be part of the most successful team in the organisation.

Step 5: Focus on "process" as well as "content"

Effective process management is essential to ensure team development.

Here's a summary:

Content is the "what" the team is trying to achieve – the goals	Process is the "how" the team works together to achieve their goals
Every team is greatly (and rightly) concerned with what they have to achieve (content). So, often a lot of time is spent (particularly at team meetings) discussing problems, issues, challenges with the tasks and projects the team is working on. However, often very little time is spent on assessing, monitoring or evaluating how effectively the team is working together (process) in order to achieve the task (content).	Teams that regularly spend time managing their process, perform better over the long term. Why? Teams that are good process managers are good at: • time keeping • giving one another feedback • involving everyone • taking account of individual differences • summarising and evaluating the progress they are making • sharing and taking leadership when it is needed • separating content from process • identifying and labelling key issues • managing conflict • making decisions • gaining commitment to group decisions

Read the above list again. How much of your team time is currently taken up with

- Content management?
- Process management?

How much better would your team perform if there was even a little more time devoted to process management? For instance, how often following a team meeting does the team assess how effectively it has performed the necessary processes? (e.g. time keeping, feedback, summarising, involving everyone, managing conflict and so on)

How do you get started with team building?

In addition to some of the points mentioned above that you can implement immediately (e.g. daily, look for someone doing something well and praise them for it) , plan and run a workshop (preferably off site) to set the tone for engagement and to gain commitment.

Following is the Team Leader's Health Check-Up together with an outline of a team development workshop that embodies all three of the engagement principles – "defining the contest", "getting team members to pledge their commitment" and "providing engrossing challenges".

HOW TO IMPLEMENT THE IDEAS IN THIS CHAPTER

☞ **How to start your development as a team leader straight away**

Undertake the *Team Leader's Health Check-Up*.

1. Please read the following list of team leader activities and rank each one.
2. Then, select the three most important for you for developing your team.
3. Complete an action plan for implementing your top three priorities and enter these actions and dates in your diary.
4. Tell your team about your three priorities and when you intend to implement them.

To develop my team, I need to …	Importance for me:		
	High	**Medium**	**Low**
A. Look for differences amongst team members and encourage these.	☐	☐	☐
B. Evaluate the strengths and weaknesses of each team member. Assign tasks accordingly.	☐	☐	☐
C. Arrange for various team members to coach and/or mentor one another. I need to make this a formal part of the team structure.	☐	☐	☐
D. Establish trust with each team member and develop an atmosphere of trust within the team by doing what I say I will do.	☐	☐	☐
E. Get results quickly. I will therefore look to the most experienced member to get the runs on the board for the team.	☐	☐	☐
F. Introduce my team to other parts of the business both socially and in writing.	☐	☐	☐
G. Distribute a short bio on each person to other parts of the organisation (and get them to write it) together with a photo.			
H. Encourage all team members to work together on projects (even if some members have a small role to play such as note taker).	☐	☐	☐
I. Gather ideas for my long term plan for the team. Discuss my plan with the team, Gather ideas. Refine my plan. Run the plan past the team members. Finalise my plan.	☐	☐	☐
J. Remember to celebrate team wins with some form of social get-together.	☐	☐	☐
K. Remember to review team failures with the team and get their ideas on how to do it better next time.	☐	☐	☐
L. Remember team member's birthdays so that we can have a small celebration.	☐	☐	☐
M. Avoid playing one team member off against another.	☐	☐	☐
N. Avoid isolating any member for any reason.	☐	☐	☐
O. Regularly run team meetings to ensure everyone is up to date and involved with team projects.	☐	☐	☐
P. Regularly review the effectiveness of the process we use to run our team meetings.	☐	☐	☐

The three top priorities for me are:	To implement these, I will ...	By (date) ...
1.		
2.		
3.		

 How to develop yourself as a team leader to your full potential and maintain team work

1. If you have not already done so, conduct "The Ideal Organisation" workshop, preferably off-site. Refer to the end of Chapter 1 for full details of how to run this workshop.

2. Once you have run the Ideal Organisation workshop and you are implementing the items on your Action List, then you are well on your way as a team leader. The team should also be starting to develop real team work.

3. Approximately, two months following the Ideal Organisation workshop and depending on the implementation of items on your Action List, conduct a follow-up workshop. This should take about two hours and could be titled *"Us as the Ideal Team. How are we progressing?"*

4. Issue pre-work about one week prior to this follow-up workshop.

5. Pre-work question could be framed:
    - Two months ago we ran the Ideal Organisation workshop and started to work on our Action Plan. How are we progressing toward our ideal? Specifically:

---

1. The aim we set for our team was to . . .

2. We now do this by . . . (things that have changed and are working)

3. The challenges we face are . . . (things that still need to happen)

4. I would rate our team as:

☐ Successful in meeting our aims
☐ Somewhat successful in meeting our aims
☐ Less than successful in meeting our

because . . . (please give specific examples that will help clarify your rating)

5. If I had to give our team a name, I would call it "(a one word adjective)"

---

6. At the meeting, start by sharing your views of the team in answer to questions 1, 2 & 3.

7. Gather your team member's views and examples from questions 1,2 & 3.

8. Write up common experiences / points on separate flipcharts headed "Q2. Things we are doing well" and "Q3. Things we still need to work on".

9. Ask people to share their ratings and their reasons (Q4)

10. Add any new items to the two flip chart lists.

11. Revisit any items on the team's original Action Plan (from the Ideal Organisation workshop) and make any necessary adjustments. Get agreement to these.

12. Share the "team names" (Q5) as a summary to the meeting.

13. Revisit the Action Plan at all future team meetings to check team development progress.

PS. You will notice, that these two workshops are an excellent way to focus on the really important process management skills mentioned in this chapter.

Chapter 4

How to Select the Right Person for the Job

Getting the essentials right

Have you ever recruited someone who looked good at the interview only to find out when they started that they "Were not up to it" or, "They just didn't seem to fit in".

Maybe you have not been involved in a selection process yet. However, even the most experienced managers have made this mistake at some time. I know I have. Why do we make these mistakes? Three reasons:

1   We often rely too much on the interview as the main selection process, or
2   We place too much emphasis on professional credentials at the expense of ability to do the job <u>and</u> a good values fit with the team, or
3   We recruit too often "in our own likeness".

What's the best way of finding out whether someone can do the job?

Try them out. The problem with an interview is that in, say half an hour discussion, you are trying to predict total behaviour and relationships for the foreseeable future.

Unfortunately, although "trying them out" is the best selection method, not everyone has the resources to be able to give someone a go. Unless of course you are recruiting for a position such as Air Traffic Controller. As a regular flyer, I know that I would be worried if the recruitment process for Air Traffic Controllers relied principally on the interview. Having now worked with a number of Air Traffic Controllers, I rest easy (and you can too) knowing that a major part of their selection process is the simulation of actual flight control.

So, if you have the resources, go for simulation. It's the next best thing to actually trying someone out on the job.

Without simulations, we must still rely on the interview. Unfortunately, numerous studies suggest that the interview by itself, is an ineffective selection method. Why? Let me pose the question – "How similar is a selection interview to the type of work the person is expected to do?"

If interviewing is not a major part of the normal day to day activities of the position for which you are recruiting, then the selection interview is not replicating the work – it's not even getting close to simulation. It's merely a discussion on what the person has done or might be able to do. Take for example the following questions, often asked at interview:

- *Tell me about your duties in your last position.*
- *What did you like most about the job?*
- *What did you like least about the job?*
- *Why do you want this job?*
- *Where do you want to be five years from now?*
- *How do you feel about working for a demanding boss?*
- *What is your management [or marketing etc] philosophy?*
- *What would you do if you were working for a manager who refuses to set priorities for you?*
- *Tell me what you would do in your first few weeks in this role.*

Now, before you reach for your pen to jot down a "new one" you liked, let me make a point. Not one of these questions works. None of them helps predict future behaviour in the job for which you are recruiting. Do any of them replicate or simulate your work situation? Unlikely.

So, how can you improve the interview?

Use Behaviour Description Interviewing

A technique known as "Behaviour Description (or Behaviour Event) Interviewing (BDI)" has been shown to improve interview effectiveness by as much as four times. Mind you, you should still use more than just the interview, but more of that later.

Read the following BDI question asked of a candidate applying for a supervisory position. One of the job requirements of the position has been identified as: "managing poor performance". See how it differs from the previous list of questions in the normal interview:

- *Tell me about the last time you faced the situation of an employee who wasn't performing.*
  - *What was the situation?*
  - *How did you deal with it?*
  - *What did you do?*
  - *What did you say?*
  - *What did he/she say?*
  - *How did you respond?*
  - *What was the outcome?*

By comparison to our previous questions, BDI asks for:

- examples of **past behaviour** that the candidate has experienced, that are likely to indicate how the candidate might perform in similar situations in the current position.

It specifically calls for:

- the description of events (i.e. behaviour – what the person said and did),
- not thoughts, feelings or hypotheses.

Additionally, it prevents the candidate from lying or exaggerating as the subsequent parts of the question will soon catch them out.

So, the BDI interviewing process becomes:

69

Now, you might be thinking "Well, that sounds ok when the applicant has actually had some experience. But what if he or she is straight out of school, university or college?"

The process still works. However you do have to be a little more creative with your questioning.

To demonstrate, let's return to the "Supervisor applicant" situation. Suppose that you have a graduate applicant who has no supervisory experience. You could ask some of the following questions:

- *I appreciate that you may not have had any formal supervisory experience yet. However, I'm sure that during your school, college or university studies you have been involved in project teams. Being part of a project team as a member or perhaps the leader, requires that you often have to get others to do things for you. Tell me about a time when you faced the situation of a team member who wasn't performing and whom you had to do something about.*
  o *What was the situation?*
  o *How did you deal with it?*
  o *What did you do?*
  o *What did you say?*
  o *What did he/she say?*
  o *How did you respond?*
  o *What was the outcome?*

Alternatively, you could relate the situation to sport, social or community activities, for example …

- *I appreciate that you may not have had any formal supervisory experience yet. However, I'm sure that during your school, college or university studies you have been a member of a sports team or perhaps a community group. Being part of teams as perhaps the leader, or even a member, requires that you often have to get others to do things for you. Tell me about a time when you faced the situation of a team member who wasn't performing and you had to do something about it.*
  o *What was the situation?*
  o *How did you deal with it?*
  o *What did you do?*

- *What did you say?*
- *What did he/she say?*
- *How did you respond?*
- *What was the outcome?*

The 5 Step Selection Process

To effectively implement BDI and recruit the best possible people, there are five steps to take:

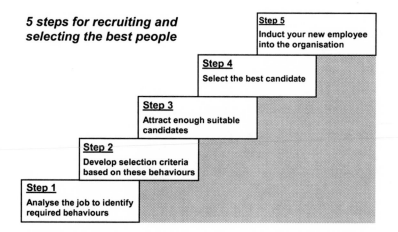

5 steps for recruiting and selecting the best people

Step 5
Induct your new employee into the organisation

Step 4
Select the best candidate

Step 3
Attract enough suitable candidates

Step 2
Develop selection criteria based on these behaviours

Step 1
Analyse the job to identify required behaviours

Step 1: Analyse the job

Because BDI calls for the candidate to describe "behaviours", it's obviously vital that we know what behaviours we are looking for. So, selecting the best applicant for the job starts with identifying the essential job behaviours.

Now, you might say "Wow, there are so many behaviours effective people display in this role. How am I going to cover all of those?" You don't have to cover all of them, just the critical ones that set an effective employee apart from an ineffective one. Think of the best operator you have seen in this field v's the worst operator. That will help you identify the behaviours you do want and those you don't want.

The best way to do this, is to ask a number of people who know most about the job;

71

- 'What are the **critical incidents** a person must handle to be successful in this role? How do they effectively handle these situations? What do they do/say when successfully handling these situations?'

Critical incidents:

- Are data not opinions, therefore they can be described
- Can be gathered from a number of sources - job holders, managers, customers etc.
- Lead directly to behaviour description questions that can be used with applicants

People who can provide this information are:

- The present jobholder (and previous ones if available)
- The manager or previous manager of this position (and other managers who have close contact)
- Staff who report to this position or who work along side the position.

Step 2: Develop your selection criteria

Here's the process to follow . . .

1. Gather examples of job holder behaviours for this position from various people (as described above).
2. Sort these examples into broad categories or areas of similar type of performance (between five and eight). Give each of these "areas of performance" a title, for example; 'Teamwork', 'Customer Service'.
3. Rank the Areas of Performance from "most" important to "least" important. This will enable you to decide which are the three most important areas of performance. The three ranked most important should be included as your essential selection criteria.
4. Within each Area of Performance, identify those behaviours which are essential. These are the behaviours the applicant must demonstrate if they are to satisfy your selection criteria for that particular Area of Performance.

5. Review the analysis undertaken so far and check it with job-holders, managers, and others for accuracy.

This analysis must be rigorous and obviously takes some time. However, when done properly, it will really help you to select the right people. A nice side benefit, is that this information can also be used to write standard operating procedures or as the basis for really effective training programs.

Here's an example for a customer service position and a BDI question . . .

Performance Area #1: CUSTOMER SERVICE	*An example of a BDI question that might be used during the interview:*
Essential (Critical) Behaviours: 1. **Is pleasant, helpful and courteous to all customers.** 2. **Anticipates the needs of customers by asking the appropriate questions.** 3. **Calls customers by name as soon as he/she identifies the customer.** 4. **Acknowledges all customers when they are waiting in the queue.**	*'I'm sure you realise how important it is to serve customers cheerfully and pleasantly. Tell me about the nicest compliment you received when serving a customer',* ● *'What did the customer want?'* ● *'Can you tell me what you said at the time?'* ● *'What did the customer say?'* ● *'Did the customer tell anyone else?'* ● *'How often did this type of event occur last year? Tell me about another one.'*

Step 3: Attract enough suitable candidates

Today, it's a very competitive market for new talent. Keep in mind that good people can pick and choose between the job you are offering and many other opportunities. We are competing in a market of low unemployment. So, how do you attract enough suitable candidates from which to make a selection?

Your best source of new talent is your existing employees. They are the ones who know your organisation well. They are also the ones who are most likely to be in contact with people who are looking for the best employer – you. They are the ones who are most likely to recommend good people to you.

Then as well, you may have internal candidates for the position. Here's a tip to keep in mind when selecting an internal candidate. We tend to choose people from outside the organisation on what they tell us that is positive about themselves. We tend to reject people from within the organisation from what we know about them that is negative. Ask yourself:

- If you were outside the organisation (e.g. a recruitment consultant) and your insider was applying for the job, how would they appear to you?

Another way to help you take a more balanced approach to internal candidates is to ask someone else (preferably someone who doesn't know the candidate very well) to assist you with the selection process. Often in public sector organisations, selection committees fill this role. Alternatively, if the role is quite senior, you may consider having an external recruitment specialist interview all candidates.

In addition to your internal candidates and people who have been recommended by your own people, there are also the recruitment agencies who can help attract and sift through the various candidates. If you use an agency, make sure you provide them with your very thorough selection criteria and that they use BDI as part of their sorting process. In this way you should only ever receive two or three candidates to interview.

Thirdly, you can advertise. Adverts need to be placed where your target audience is likely to see them. If you are looking for experienced, competent people, then you want to attract those who are already employed elsewhere, not those who are looking in the "Positions Vacant" (the best people already have jobs, unless you are looking for entry level people who have not had their first job). Advertise where current employees are likely to be reading – professional journals, websites of interest, the general news section of papers (not the "Positions Vacant") and so on.

If you do have to advertise, remember to place in your ad what your candidate might be looking for as well as what you are looking for. You are trying to attract already employed, experienced and competent people. They need to see your benefits. Many people involved in the recruitment process express their advertisements (both internal and external) only in terms of what they want in an applicant. Whilst this is very important, it is only half the story. Every recruitment ad also sells you and the organisation.

Your ads should describe what the successful applicant will get from the job. Sometimes salary and standard organisational benefits are mentioned, but what are the benefits of this particular role? Make sure you include all the benefits of working for your organisation – ask your people, they will tell you what they are.

Here's an example of a well designed job advertisement . . .

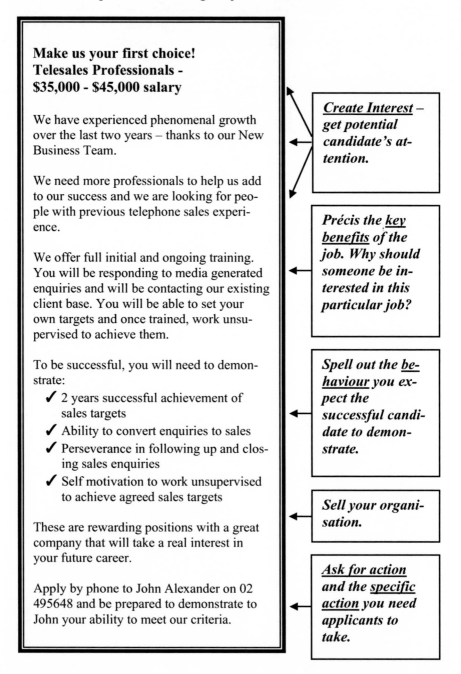

**Make us your first choice!
Telesales Professionals -
$35,000 - $45,000 salary**

We have experienced phenomenal growth over the last two years – thanks to our New Business Team.

We need more professionals to help us add to our success and we are looking for people with previous telephone sales experience.

We offer full initial and ongoing training. You will be responding to media generated enquiries and will be contacting our existing client base. You will be able to set your own targets and once trained, work unsupervised to achieve them.

To be successful, you will need to demonstrate:
- ✓ 2 years successful achievement of sales targets
- ✓ Ability to convert enquiries to sales
- ✓ Perseverance in following up and closing sales enquiries
- ✓ Self motivation to work unsupervised to achieve agreed sales targets

These are rewarding positions with a great company that will take a real interest in your future career.

Apply by phone to John Alexander on 02 495648 and be prepared to demonstrate to John your ability to meet our criteria.

Create Interest – get potential candidate's attention.

Précis the key benefits of the job. Why should someone be interested in this particular job?

Spell out the behaviour you expect the successful candidate to demonstrate.

Sell your organisation.

Ask for action and the specific action you need applicants to take.

Step 4: Select the best candidate

Here's an overview of the process.

* **Assess each applicant's answers**

During the interview, look for the behaviours that best match your examples you developed earlier as part of your job analysis. A good way of doing this is to use a form such as the following to collect your information.

INTERVIEW FORM

Applicant

Performance Area	Key Behaviours to look for
1.	•
	•
2.	•
	•
3.	•
	•

BDI Questions to ask the applicant:
1.
2.
3.

EVENT- he/she told me about ...	BEHAVIOUR they described ...	OUTCOME of the event was ...

OVERALL RATING

Finally, you need to make your choice. Here's a checklist:

☑ Which candidate meets all of your selection criteria?

☑ If none of your candidates meet all of your selection criteria, then start the recruitment process again. It's far better to be without someone for a period of time in the role than to try to manage someone who doesn't quite fit. My rule is "If in doubt, don't".

☑ If more than one candidate meets your selection criteria, consider selecting the one that has the best values fit (see below for further explanation). If you are in the luxurious position of having two ideal candidates and you find it hard to choose, ask your team – they will be the best judges because they will have to work with the successful candidate.

☑ Check references (and if necessary qualifications) – see below for further details.

Step 5: Induct your new employee

Of all the training that takes place in organisations, induction is without doubt the most important. Why? Because it is at this time that the new recruit is at his/her keenest – they have made a major life decision – to join your organisation. They want it to work out well and are looking to you to help.

The second thing about induction, is that this is the best possible time to have the person adopt your culture; to adopt a positive attitude that could remain with them for years to come.

Whether your organisation has a formal induction process, or it is left to each individual manager, the following checklist will be a good start for your induction process:

Induction Check List

1. Send a welcoming letter (in addition to the formal job offer) AND give them a phone call. You will be the key person for them in the months ahead. A positive relationship must be started and nourished.

2. Put a detailed induction and training plan in place for the next three months which covers:

   - Job Description
   - Sponsor
   - Organisation policies and procedures
   - Pay and benefits
   - Training to be undertaken
   - Staff lists
   - Organisation culture or philosophy
   - Local knowledge needed for new recruit
   - Key people they should interview during their first three months
   - Measurement of Job Performance.

3. Prepare an initial training assignment for the new recruit to complete within the first week. The assignment should relate to both their role and the organisation.

4. Involve other staff and managers in the induction plan. Set times for their involvement. Give them a copy of the plan.

5. Appoint a sponsor or mentor for the new recruit for the first three weeks. Advise the sponsor of his/her responsibilities. Give him/her a copy of the plan.

6. Discuss the induction plan with the new recruit on the first day. Give him/her a copy.

7. Diarise to follow up weekly on progress for the first three months.

Other possible recruitment tools and tips

• Tests – are they useful?

In addition to the BDI interview, what do you need to add to your selection armoury? Depending on the position, there are of course the professional qualifications, but we all know that these merely get the candidate through the gate – it's what he or she can do with their qualifications that we are interested in. For some positions, you may also decide that IQ (Intelligence Quotient) , EQ (Emotional Intelligence) or personality tests are useful. If so, these need to be shown to be reliable tests by correlation with previously successful job holders.

• References – do they work?

Then of course there's the reference. Written references are almost useless as people will only say the nice things in a written reference. Phone references are generally ineffective for the same reasons as the standard employment interview. However, you can increase the effectiveness of phone references by using the BDI method over the phone with the candidate's referee. The best referee, if it is possible and ethical to make contact, is the candidate's previous manager.

• Values fit – will the new person fit in?

In addition to finding out whether someone can do the job, there's also the very important aspect of "values fit". Will the person fit in with the people and the culture?

There are numerous values questionnaires on the market that you may try. However, there are two simple techniques that could save you money. Both of these are dependent on the fact that you already know what values you are looking for.

The first is to ask the applicant to describe their "ideal organisation". In doing so, they will always describe the values they hold dear when looking for an employer. (You will recall that we covered the Ideal Organisation in Chapter 2 – review that exercise to develop your Ideal Organisation questions)

The second is to ask your team (the people the candidate will be working alongside) to also do a short interview – this can often be achieved in conjunction with a plant or office tour.

- **Job preferences – what are they?**

There's also the aspect of how well the person is suited to the type of work involved. You may glean people's preferences from the examples they give in the BDI interviews. For example do they prefer a role that involves;

- more **quantitative** type work such as scientific/analytical, mathematical/numerate, clerical/administrative, practical/manual? or,
- more **qualitative** type work such as selling/persuasive, outdoor/mobile, creative/artistic, social/people?

If you want to do this in a more formal way, there are questionnaires available such as the Decision Preference Analysis.

- **Avoid recruiting in your own likeness – vary your team**

Finally, a word of warning. One of the most frequent mistakes I see is managers recruiting in their own likeness, i.e. people who are similar to themselves in many ways. This is a natural tendency of human nature, but can be avoided if you use the BDI method, together with your team members and perhaps peers, assisting you in the selection of the final candidate. Ask yourself:

- How much like me is this person? Is this appropriate?

Whilst it may be comfortable to work with people like yourself, my experience has been that the best managers have the most diverse teams.

If you have the opportunity to build your team from scratch, or you want to ensure there is diversity within the team, there are tools such as The Team Management Profile or Belbin's Team Roles that are useful. Both of these provide an analysis of a person's preferences for taking on various team roles.

HOW TO IMPLEMENT THE IDEAS IN THIS CHAPTER

 How to start recruiting someone straight away

Sorry folks, there are no quick and easy ways to recruit and select someone. There are no shortcuts – it's too important a task and cannot be hurried.

How to recruit and select the best people

Steps to take for effective selection	Actions required in each step
Step 1: **Analyse the job** to identify the required behaviours	• Ask people who know the job well, to identify the critical incidents that are handled well by a competent employee. • What are the behaviours that the competent employee uses when satisfactorily handling these critical incidents?
Step 2: **Develop your selection criteria** based on the above behaviours	• Categorise these critical incidents into broad Areas of Performance (5-8 only) and give each area a name. • Rank the Areas of Importance from most to least important. • Within each Area of Importance, identify the essential behaviours the candidate must display.
Step 3: **Attract enough suitable candidates**	• Ask your people to introduce good candidates. • Advertise. • Use advertising or recruitment agencies.
Step 4: **Select** the **best** candidate	• Assess each candidate's answers against your selection criteria.
Step 5: **Induct your new employee** – plan the induction thoroughly	• Phone and send out a welcoming letter.

	• Develop an induction and training plan.
	• Set a training assignment.
	• Involve other staff in the induction plan.
	• Appoint a sponsor.
	• Give a copy of the plan to your new employee on the first day.
	• Follow up progress weekly.

Chapter 5

How to set Performance Standards for your people

Role clarity – the key to managing performance

There are two steps to setting performance standards for your people:

- Step 1: Clearly define each person's role
- Step 2: Set and agree performance standards and measures

Step 1: Clearly define each person's role

Bob's Case: Role conflict

I once applied for a job as a Training Manager in a dynamic and rapidly developing organisation. My application was successful and I was delighted to find out that one of my current colleagues would be joining me in the new organisation. He and I got on very well together at work and we also had a good personal relationship - we occasionally had barbecues at one another's homes. Apparently and unbeknown to one another, we had both applied for the same role as Training Manager.

The organisation liked us both and as they were expanding rapidly, they employed both of us. Because they now had two people where originally they were only looking for one, they designated my role as "Senior Training Manager" and his as "Training Manager". He would report to me. Over barbecue discussions prior to starting in our new roles, we both said how much we were looking forward to working together in this new and exciting environment.

A couple of weeks into our new roles, my friend and I were starting to have some differences. By the end of three months, these differences had escalated to conflict. Why? We liked one another, got on well together both socially and as work colleagues in our previous organisation. We also shared very similar views on the role of the training function.

The problem lay not in our relationship, but in the "how" the training function was to be managed – I had my views and he had his. Our new organisation had developed Position Descriptions for each of our new roles. However, they were written in "input" terms – i.e., the sorts of things we were expected to do and how we should do things, rather than "output" terms, i.e. the results each of us was expected to achieve. As a result, there was major overlap in role descriptions and so our dis-agreements became "role conflict".

Now, my experience may seem like an extreme case. Let me assure you that it's not. It is not always clear when you are in the middle of a role conflict situation. Very often we confuse it as a personality conflict, which it is definitely not.

As a new manager, unless you are very clear about:

- defining your team member's roles and
- your expectations of each person in the role,

then misunderstandings can lead to poor or misguided performance. At worst, these misunderstandings may end up in major role conflict.

1.1 Define the role of each team member in outputs not inputs

One of the real problems with Position Descriptions (PDs) is that they are often written in Input terms (i.e. what people do,) for example:

– *"Supervise and direct the operations of the customer service team"*

rather than Outputs (i.e. what **people achieve**). For example:

– *"Ensure customer satisfaction is assured".*

When PDs are written in input terms, there are three possible results.

Firstly, there is a better than average chance that there will be overlap or under lap between team member's roles. It's virtually impossible to write down everything that has to be done.

Secondly, people may stick rigidly to what they are expected to do. This often means they become narrow minded, rather than looking at the bigger picture - what they need to achieve for the betterment of their team and ultimately, the organisation.

Finally, the input-oriented PD may be used as alibi paper. For example, in larger organisations, particularly where there is a culture of rigid hierarchy, use of input oriented PDs invariably leads to conflict. The PD is then called upon as alibi paper when something that should have been achieved, slips through the cracks. "That's not on my PD". Even the best written PDs will not cover all eventualities. That's why the focus on outputs is so important. In smaller organisations, PDs written in input terms can lead to a feeling of being overworked. People end up saying things like "this is not my responsibility" when the person is asked to do something that is not specifically written into their PD.

1.2 Use the process of writing the PD in collaboration with your team member to gain their commitment

You should use the PD and in particular the writing of the PD, as a process of reaching agreement between yourself and your team member as to what the role should achieve.

As a new manager, it is the **process** of discussing and agreeing output areas with your team members that is critical for effective working relationships, job design and ultimately organisation structure. It is not the piece of paper that the PD ends up on.

PDs should not be written in isolation by one person, nor should they be written by the HR Department. If the HR Department is involved in writing PDs, their role should be to coach, train and facilitate the writers – i.e. the people who will be doing the actual work - you and your team members. Above all, PDs should not be copied out of one of the many books available with pre-written position descriptions. If a person is going to do the job, they need to think through what it is that they are required to achieve in that job.

1.3 Turn inputs into outputs by adding "so that . . . "

How do you write effective Position Descriptions that are expressed in output terms? One way is to convert existing PDs. For example, look at the following list of duties from the Supervisor's PD at a large main frame computer centre:

1. Supervise and direct the operations of the computer room in a large scale, multi mainframe operations environment.
2. Provide on-the-job training aides for operating staff to ensure the standard operations procedures are maintained.
3. Provide assistance in the analysis and correction of systems hardware, software and production failures and/or notify appropriate personnel.
4. Maintain computer usage records and operational logs.
5. Deputise for the shift manager.

All of the above are expressed as "inputs" rather than "outputs"   If they were expressed as outputs, they would be written as:

INPUTS	OUTPUTS *An Input is turned into an Output by adding "so that . . . " and completing the sentence, or asking "Why?"*
1. Supervise and direct the operations of the computer room in a large scale, multi mainframe operations environment	• Mainframe down time is minimal • Quality output standard of data is maintained • All staff meet their performance standards
2. Provide on-the-job training aides for operating staff to ensure the standard operations procedures are maintained	• Standard operating procedures always followed • Errors are minimised • Problems solved within specified time and quality standards
3. Provide assistance in the analysis and correction of systems hardware, software and production failures and/or notify appropriate personnel	
4. Maintain computer usage records and operational logs	
5. Deputise for the shift manager	

So, as you can see, it's very simple to turn inputs into outputs - just add "so that . . . " to each input and complete the sentence. Or, another easy way of doing it is to ask "Why?" of each input and keep asking "Why?" until the answer becomes an output.

You may like to try your hand at rewriting inputs 3, 4 & 5 above.

As you do, you will notice that outputs start to repeat themselves fairly frequently. That's because outputs focus on the results not "how" the job is done. It often takes several inputs to achieve an output. Output-oriented PDs will usually be much shorter than the list of inputs required to achieve those outputs. Although "how" is important, it can be stated later when you complete Step 2 with your team member "Set and agree performance standards and measures". For now and for role clarity, the focus must remain on getting the outputs identified.

Most PDs written in output terms will end up with no more than five or six outputs. For lower level roles, this can rise to as many as eight to ten (although be careful that none of these become inputs). The general rule of thumb for the number of outputs is:

–   *"The more senior the role, the less number of outputs a manager should have".*

So, for example by the time you get to the CEO's role there is only one output that he or she must achieve – "Stakeholder expectations managed effectively"

Remember as I said earlier, it is the process of discussing and agreeing output areas that is critical for effective working relationships, job design and ultimately organisation structure, not the piece of paper that the PD ends up on. So make sure the people doing the work are involved in writing the PDs.

Note: If you do not currently have any PDs for your team members, you can still use a similar approach. Just ask each team member to list all their duties or responsibilities, then take them through the process of turning these duties or responsibilities into outputs. You will be surprised at how quickly people learn to do this.

A nice by-product of identifying the outputs for each team member's role, is that they provide the basis for results oriented training modules. So for example, a training module titled "Guarantee Customer Satisfaction" (output) might be quite different and potentially far more effective than one titled "Provide Customer Service" (input).

Oh, by the way, you may be wondering what eventually happened between my colleague and I that I mentioned at the start of the chapter. He applied for a role elsewhere in the organisation – his old role was not re-filled. Both I and the organisation had learned about "outputs" by that stage.

Step 2: Set and agree performance standards and measures

Now that you have the outputs established for your team member's role, it is a simple matter to set the required performance standards.

2.1   Always involve the team member in setting his or her own performance standards

Once again, it is vitally important that your team members are involved in this critical element of managing performance. If they are involved from the outset, there is far less managing required of you. You will find that they will take more responsibility for achieving the standards they have helped set.

2.2 Conduct a separate performance meeting with each team member

You should have an individual meeting with each of your team members to set and agree their performance standards.

Ask each team member to take their list of outputs and add performance measures to them. They can do this by simply answering the question "When I am achieving this output, what should I see happening as a result?", or "How would I know when I am achieving this output?" Their answers should include measures that are stated in terms of:

- **Quantity** - i.e. How many?
- **Quality** - i.e. What standard is achieved?
- **Time** – i.e By When?
- **Cost or Revenue** – i.e. How much?

For example . . .

Input	Output	Measured in terms of: Quantity, Quality, Time and / or Cost / Revenue
1. Supervise and direct the operations of the computer room in a large scale, multi mainframe operations environment.	• Mainframe down time is minimal. • Quality output standard of data is maintained. • All staff meet their performance standards.	• System is operational 24/7 with the exception of 1 hour monthly maintenance. • System is restored within 30 minutes of malfunction on all occasions. • Input of data is 100% accurate and able to be retrieved immediately. • Performance standards set with staff are achievable and met within the time and quality requirements.
2. Provide on-the-job training aides for operating staff to ensure the standard operations procedures are maintained.	• Standard operating procedures followed. • Errors are minimised. • Problems solved within specified time and quality standards.	• Error free audits achieved. • Errors are corrected immediately. • Customers are advised of problems immediately, setting out time frame for solutions which are adhered to in 100% of cases.

Clarifying each team member's role, then setting and agreeing their performance standards will make your role as a new manager so much easier. Using this approach you are more likely to gain each team member's **commitment** to achieving the required performance standards. Managers who try to enforce their performance standards without taking this collaborative approach, at best obtain **compliance.**

As a manager, I would like my people to be committed rather than compliant, wouldn't you?

HOW TO IMPLEMENT THE IDEAS IN THIS CHAPTER

 How to start setting Performance Standards straight away

The quick and easy way, is to:

- Copy this chapter of the book and have each of your team members read it
- Conduct a team meeting to clarify roles
- Have an individual meeting with each team member to agree the performance standards required

How to fully get your people committed to achieving their performance standards.

Implement the following action plan

 Your plan of action – activities, dates, people to involve

Step	Date to imple-ment	Action to take	People to involve	Follow-up date	Follow-up action
1.		• Conduct a team meeting to introduce the concept of outputs and clearly define each person's role in output terms. • At the meeting, turn inputs into outputs by adding "so that …"	• Self and team		• Publish the PDs or Role Descriptions. • Have each team member start work on setting their performance standards.
2.		• Set and agree performance standards with each team member. • Make sure that each output has standards that can be measured and assessed in terms of: Quantity, Quality, Time and Cost / Revenue.	• Self with each team member individually		• Regularly check with each team member to ensure standards are met. • At least quarterly, review each team member's performance.

Chapter 6

How to Motivate Others

There's an old saying; "You can't motivate somebody. You can only provide the conditions within which they can motivate themselves."

Have you been appreciated lately?

1.   The first step to motivating others – *recognition*

We all like to be associated with a winner, be it a winning person, a winning team, a worthwhile cause or a successful organisation. We all have sports people, teams, actors or artists that we consider "ours". When they do well, we bask in the reflected glory of their achievements. It's the same at work - we want to be associated with a worthwhile, winning organisation. Our greatest reward is receiving acknowledgment that we have contributed to making something meaningful happen. More than anything else, people want to be valued for a job well done by those they hold in high regard.

A famous study by Lawrence Lindahl in the 1940's came up with some surprising results. When supervisors and their employees were asked to list "What motivates the employees?"

- **Employees** listed "appreciation of a job well done" as number one and "feeling in on things" as number two.
- **Supervisors**, on the other hand, expected the employees would rank these two items as eighth and tenth respectively. Supervisors thought employees would put wages as number one, job security as number two and promotion as number three.

Lindahl's full list shows . . .

Factors managers & employees were asked to rank . . .	Manager's Ranking	Employee's Ranking
Full appreciation for work done	8	1
Good wages	1	5
Good working conditions	4	9
Interesting work	5	6
Job security	2	4
Promotion / Growth opportunities	3	7
Personal loyalty to workers	6	8
Feeling "In" on things	10	2
Sympathetic help on personal problems	9	3
Tactful disciplining	7	10

These results were replicated in similar studies in the 1980's and again in the 1990's. In another recent study, employees were asked to rank job-based incentives – "a personal thank-you" came first and "a note of appreciation from my manager" came second. "Money" came in at 16th!

Praise, the thing that motivates us the most, takes so little time and yet costs nothing. As the famous management writer Rosabeth Moss Kantor once said *"Compensation is a right. Recognition is a gift."*

As a new manager, has the value of your work been appreciated recently? Have you appreciated the work of others? Here's a quick test. Over the last week, have you:

- ☐ Told someone they have done a good job?
- ☐ Looked specifically to find someone doing something well?
- ☐ Made someone else look good rather than taking the credit yourself?
- ☐ Thanked others for your own success?
- ☐ Passed on positive comments you have heard about others?

These are simple examples of the things you need to do regularly to acknowledge the good work of others.

You might say, "If it's that easy, why don't more people do it?" There are many reasons, but they all fall into two categories – personal and organisational.

On a personal level, many of us are not comfortable giving praise. We may be awkward about it, or perhaps believe that people are paid to do a job, so why do we have to praise them?

From an organisational perspective, it may be the culture that is holding us back, or perhaps technology preventing us from valuing the work of others. For example, technology has changed the way many of us operate. Email may have replaced personal interaction, so we no longer see what others do well – out of sight is out of mind, so how can we praise good work if we don't see it?

Here are six ways you can put praise for a job well done back into your working life and at the same time help motivate your people:

1.	*Look for things people do well and acknowledge them for their good work.*
2.	*Be a model of acknowledgment – show others it's OK to give praise.*
3.	*Have a conversation with a fellow manager about how to give praise for work well done (this will be challenging, but highly rewarding).*
4.	*When your people have performed above the norm, write them a small thank you note.*
5.	*Encourage your people to thank one another and pass on stories of good work to you. Pass on these good work stories to your manager.*
6.	*Work to create a culture of appreciation – make acknowledgment part of your daily routine.*

The essential point is that praise must be frequent and given locally by you and your colleagues. It should not be a corporate initiative or program, but simply "the way we do things around here".

Above all, praise must be genuine. People in general are very good at spotting insincerity. The message? When you do praise someone, make sure it's for the good work they have done and not just for the sake of it.

So, find someone doing something good today and simply tell them what a good job they've done.

2. In addition to recognition, what else motivates people?

When was the last time you felt excited, motivated and extremely keen to be at work? Chances are it was when you had a job or project that really interested you, you had control over what you did and the way you did it, and you didn't have any worries about "over zealous boss" interference or lack of job security. It's a great feeling and we can all probably relate stories of how and when we were most motivated at work.

But as a manager, do you consciously try to provide this same level of motivation for all of your employees?

Experience suggests that because managers are so busy, they tend to forget what it was really like when they worked in an environment that was truly motivational.

My challenge to you, is to:

- Think back to when you were most motivated at work
- Identify the reasons why
- List these reasons on a sheet of paper as dot points
- Set about implementing these same conditions for your own people

I've issued this challenge to managers over the last 20 years in management development forums and invariably they identify the following. Are some of your motivators similar to theirs?

- Autonomy – the chance to take control over a complete project or unit of work in which I am really interested
- Responsibility – for setting goals and targets and being accountable for achieving them
- Recognition – for achieving meaningful results
- Development – of my skills, knowledge and capabilities to their full potential

I then ask them to identify the things that really irritate and annoy them and often change what could have been a motivating workplace into a drudgery. The things they come up with are:

- Bosses who do not recognise me for my efforts, or worse still, take the credit themselves
- A lack of feeling of "team", instead of "we are in this together"
- Constant implied threats of demotion or dismissal
- Insufficient salary by comparison to others in the firm or in the industry

Frederick Herzberg in his classic HBR article "One More Time, How do you Motivate Employees?" (harvardbusinessonline.hbsp.harvard.edu) came up with two similar sets of lists nearly forty years ago that he labeled "Motivators" and "Satisfiers".

Motivators	Satisfiers
• Achievement • Recognition for achievement • Meaningful interesting work • Responsibility • Opportunity for personal growth and development	• Money • Supervision • Working conditions

3. Focus on both the "motivators" and the "satisfiers"

Motivators and satisfiers are equally important. One is not more or less important than the other. Motivators do in fact keep people motivated. However, motivated people can quickly become dissatisfied if they feel that any of the satisfiers is not right or is diminished in any way. For example, when highly motivated people's salary or job security is threatened, they become quite dissatisfied even though all of the motivators may still be present.

Put another way, satisfiers take people up to a neutral level. If they are absent people go negative. But providing more and more satisfiers won't get people to go positive. Only the motivators will take people above the neutral level.

```
┌─────────────────────────────────────────┐
│ Positive employees                       │
└─────────────────────────────────────────┘
              ⬆
         The Motivators

┌─────────────────────────────────────────┐
│ Neutral                                  │
└─────────────────────────────────────────┘
                              ⬆
                       The Satisfiers

┌─────────────────────────────────────────┐
│ Negative employees                       │
└─────────────────────────────────────────┘
```

As a manager. you must address and continually manage, both the motivators and the satisfiers if you are to have motivated people.

Take another look at the lists of things that managers in my forums came up with. You will notice that all of the five motivators are there when these managers were asked about their "most motivating work experiences". On the other hand, two of the three satisfiers – money and supervision – were on their list of things that most irritated them when these were not right.

- **A word of warning. Be careful not to overstate or over emphasise the satisfiers, particularly at the expense of the motivators**

It's very tempting to say that money motivates people. Money is important to keep people satisfied, but it does not motivate them.

"Oh, yeah" I hear you say, "money certainly motivates me".

Let me pose a question to you: "If I were to double your pay today, would you work any better than you are working now?" You may be a lot more enthusiastic (well, at least for the first week). My guess is that you are currently working to the best of your ability right now. Giving you the extra money may be very satisfying and make you feel good, but it will not motivate you to work any harder or better. You probably can't.

Do Herzberg's motivators and satisfiers hold true today? Recent research into the turnover rates for young employees (20 – 30 yrs) shows that in some industries, the turnover rate of young employees is as high as 25% annually. This is due to lack of perceived career development and training and limited opportunities for involvement in other areas of the firm and their profession. These younger people, by comparison to their predecessors:

- Are more opportunistic in taking new jobs.
- Are more mobile.
- Have greater expectations.
- Are easily bored.

So, it would seem that Herzberg's motivators and satisfiers are even more important for the new manager to work on today. Today's younger employee is not so different from the generation who manage them – maybe they just want their motivation and satisfaction a little faster!

HOW TO IMPLEMENT THE IDEAS IN THIS CHAPTER

➤ How to start Motivating your people straight away

1. Catch people out doing well and acknowledge them for their good work.
2. Be a model of acknowledgment – show others it's OK to give praise.
3. Have a conversation with a fellow manager about how to give praise for work well done.
4. When your people have performed above the norm, write them a small thank you note.
5. Encourage your people to thank one another and pass on stories of good work to you. Pass on these good work stories to your manager.
6. Work to create a culture of appreciation – make acknowledgment part of your daily routine.

👉 How to get your people fully motivated

Introduce / Build on the Motivators	Actions to take . . .
• Develop a real sense of **ACHIEVEMENT** in your people	• Make sure your people are able to measure and / or assess their own performance against set standards. • Be serious about performance reviews.
• Increase the amount and quality of **RECOGNITION** you give then for their achievements	• Revisit the list of "How to start motivating your people straight away" and start implementing these. • Make a note in your diary to praise at least one of your team members for a job well done, every day.
• Increase the amount and degree of **RESPONSIBILITY** you give them	• Create a forum to develop a greater spirit of involvement with the challenges facing your team and your people. • Encourage your people to take more initiative (see also the chapter on "Delegation").
• Develop their work or role so that it is more **MEANINGFUL** and **INTERESTING** to them	• Try to ensure people are responsible for an entire job or process, not a part. • Encourage people to meet and interact with their ultimate customers. This gives their job a sense of meaning. • Provide job rotation.
• Increase their opportunity for **GROWTH** and **ADVANCEMENT**	• Be honest when talking about career and development opportunities. • Do more career mapping. • Spend time training and developing your people. • Identify and encourage some of your team members to coach their colleagues.

How to ensure your people remain satisfied with their pay, supervision and working conditions

Maintain the Satisfiers	Actions to take . . .
• Ensure your people are aware of the relevance of their **SALARY**	• Publicise salary ranges in relation to jobs. • If salary ranges are out of kilter with the work requirements or they do not match industry standards, work with your HR people to rectify the situation. If necessary, ask the HR people to get a specialist to do a proper job evaluation.
• Ensure your people are happy with their **SUPERVISION**	• Be honest in all your dealings with your people. • Set an example by doing what you say you will do.
• Monitor **WORKING CONDITIONS**	• Ensure working conditions are the best they can be. • Ensure safety standards are set and maintained. • Develop forums for social interaction both inside and outside of work.

Chapter 7

How to give Feedback – Positive and Negative

Is there a better way to give bad news?

Bob's Case: The impact of inappropriate feedback

I well remember the first time I was "corrected" by a manager. I was a young bank clerk and had received a transaction that was incorrect, from a much more senior person, a manager, in another branch of the bank. I sent the transaction back with a note asking for it to be corrected. Next thing I hear was my own manager shouting at me from his office. Apparently, I had upset his good colleague and I must now go and apologise in person! There was no discussion as to whether I was right or wrong about either the transaction or what I did – just "Go immediately and apologise!" I decided then and there that when I got to be a manager and had to correct someone, I would treat my staff quite differently.

As managers, we all have to give feedback from time to time that we consider to be bad news for the employee.

- Do you dread the times when you have to do this?
- Or perhaps, you handle the situation ok, but the employee's performance does not seem to improve as a result of your counseling?

Yes, you'll be pleased to know, there is a better way to give bad news!

Of course, there are also the times when we give, or probably more to the point, we SHOULD give positive feedback. You will recall that this was mentioned in the previous chapter with the idea "catch somebody out doing a good job".

- Do you do this often enough?
- Does it have the impact that you would like it to have?

Whether it's positive or negative feedback that you need to give, there are six rules that apply. Following these six rules will increase the effectiveness of your feedback.

The six rules for giving feedback – both positive and negative

---

1. **Get straight to the point**
2. **Keep good news and bad news separate**
3. **Use "I" messages and avoid using "You"**
4. **Criticise or praise the act, not the person**
5. **Give examples of behaviour and why it is causing you pain or pleasing you**
6. **Reinforce "best" behaviour. Let the person know when they have met or exceeded your standards and when they have not**

Rule 1: Get straight to the point

I remember some years ago, a colleague of mine Stuart, telling me about the time his boss called he and two of his work mates into his office for a "chat". Stuart said to me *"I knew right from the start that we were there to be hauled over the coals. But the boss kept saying how well things were going in general, how hard everyone was working at the moment, what challenges we were all facing and so on. By the time he got to what he really wanted to say, I wasn't interested. More to the point I didn't want to listen, I just wanted to get back to work."*

I was curious about how Stuart knew that he and his colleagues were there to be criticised right from the start of the conversation. He said to me *"Bob, it wasn't what he said so much, although he did seem to waffle on forever, it was his body language and what he was not saying that gave it away. I just knew."*

Waffling or padding the feedback message detracts from the actual message. Whether you know it or not, your people will know why you are speaking to them – they will just "know".

Here's one way Stuart's boss could have started the conversation more effectively:

"Thanks for taking a few moments of your time. This is rather difficult for me, so I'll get straight to the point. I have been disappointed with one particular aspect of the current project outcomes this week."

This direct approach ensures that everyone is focused on the topic of the conversation, not extraneous matters.

<u>Rule 2</u>: Keep bad news and good news separate

The most common mistake we make when giving feedback, particularly negative feedback, is combining bad news with good news – i.e. what the person is doing well and not so well. This is often called the "feedback sandwich" – give good, bad, good. Take a look at the following example.

Andrew and the Feedback Sandwich

"Andrew, I've been impressed with the way you handle the planning, time lines and follow up systems for your projects. But, along the way, you seem to develop poor relationships with some of the key stakeholders. As a result, many of your projects are less successful than they should be. On the other hand, your projects always come in on time."

On the surface, this sounds like a reasonable feedback message from the manager. Will Andrew accept the feedback? Is it likely to lead to a rational discussion of how he might improve his stakeholder relationships?

No. There are three reasons why the conversation between Andrew and his manager is likely to be ineffective.

- **People hear the "good" more than the "bad"**

Firstly, when mixing good and bad news, people are more likely to hear only the good news. The bad news, if heard, appears as a minor blimp on their performance chart. In their mind, "everything is basically ok with me and what I do".

Keeping bad news and good news separate means just that – when you want to criticise something that someone has done, say so. Do not sugar coat it with lots of things that the person has done well. I've often heard (inexperienced) managers say that when criticising people, you should give good news – bad news – good news. Believe me feedback sandwiches are inedible!

When positive and negative feedback are given together, people are far more likely to remember only the positive. So, if your intention is to give some negative feedback with the aim of improving your employee's performance, keep the message clear and clean.

However, although the feedback itself may be negative this does not mean that the tone of your message has to be negative. In fact it can be quite a positively toned feedback statement. For example, "Sandy, these reports are incomplete. You're usually very thorough with your reports. Can you tell me why these particular reports are incomplete?"

Your aim should always be to maintain your employee's self-esteem and reduce defensiveness, whilst staying focused on the specific problem. Notice that the feedback to Sandy above, is quite different from the "feedback sandwich" mentioned earlier. In this case there is a positive statement – about the person and there is a negative statement – about this specific piece of behaviour.

If you are still concerned that only giving bad news may be too difficult for you, here's a suggestion that may ease the pressure. Talk about your positive feelings for the person and perhaps the team in your introduction. You could start with something such as:

"I care about your success, and the success of our team. That's why I wanted to talk with you today."

Above all, when you are preparing your feedback message, remember to keep it clear, simple and direct – people can only improve if they know where they are currently not performing well.

- **Avoid the "But" word**

Secondly, when good and bad news is mixed and the person does actually hear the bad news, it is nearly always because the word "but" has been used to bridge the good and the bad. Using "but" will invariably promote a negative reaction from the employee and the conversation will degenerate into a downward spiral of argument and counter argument.

"But" immediately lessens any good news that may have been given and in fact generally infers criticism, or at the very least an opposing view. Read the Andrew message again, this time put your name where Andrew's was – see how you feel when the "but" message is aimed directly at you . . .

How do you feel when given a "but" message?

"(Put your own name here ... ...), I've been impressed with the way you handle the planning, time lines and follow up systems for your projects. But, along the way, you seem to develop poor relationships with some of the key stakeholders. As a result, many of your projects are less successful than they should be"

- **Avoid "You"**

Thirdly, avoid the use of the word "You", particularly to describe past behaviour. "You" infers criticism of the person as well as the act. What we want to do is to give some critical feedback of what the person <u>did</u>, not the person.

Because the "You" message implies criticism, when used as part of the feedback process it triggers the person's natural fight or flight defense mechanism. They either become quite angry or aggressive, or retreat into themselves. As a result, they tend not to accept the feedback.

If you want proof of the impact of the "you" word, think for a moment about the last time you had a major disagreement or argument with a loved one. I'd put money on the fact that the word that was thrown around by both of you more than any other, was "you"! Am I right?

As you think about your own loved-one situation, take a look at the actual words a supervisor used when criticising a customer service person in an organisation where I once worked:

How not to give feedback – the case of the "You" supervisor

"You are disorganized and as a result you don't get the work through on time. You don't seem to be really interested in getting the right results. You don't follow instructions at all well. You make too many silly mistakes in the balancing and I don't think you are really suited to the Customer Service role."

How would you feel if you received feedback in that way? This is how the customer service person actually responded:

"I am not disorganized. I keep my desk clean for the benefit of the customers. Any mistakes I make are quickly corrected. As for my being suitable for the role, I am very customer oriented. Any uncertainty I show is not because of my skills but because of the way instructions are given. If instructions were given in a positive way by you and not as criticism, then I would be better at my job."

One can almost hear the steam coming out of the customer service person's mouth, nose and ears! Look once again at the words the supervisor used – you'll see the impact that the supervisor's "you" had on the customer service person:

"<u>You</u> are disorganized and as a result <u>you</u> don't get the work through on time. <u>You</u> don't seem to be really interested in getting the right results. <u>You</u> don't follow instructions at all well. <u>You</u> make too many silly mistakes in the balancing and I don't think <u>you</u> are really suited to the Customer Service role."

Here's a test for "you". Next time you get into an argument or heated discussion with a loved one, try not using the word "you" at all. This will be extremely hard at first. Stick with it and see the impact it has on the conversation. You will be amazed at how your own heated emotional level drops, your message becomes clearer and the conversation becomes more rational and productive. You will probably still have your differences, only now they will be able to be discussed far more sanely and calmly.

<u>Rule 3</u>: Use "I" messages rather than "You" messages

Could the message by the supervisor to the customer service person been given in a way that would have been accepted?

Yes. The answer is to avoid "You" and use "I" messages instead. Here's an approach the supervisor could have used:

A better way to give feedback

"Sue, thanks for taking a moment of your time to talk with me. I'm only new to the role of supervisor, so I feel a bit uncomfortable with this. Please bear with me. I've noticed over the last two weeks that your batch work has not been getting through on time. This seems unusual to me, as it's normally ok. Has anything changed over the last two weeks that might have led to these delays?"

Using "I messages" is such an important rule, that below are some examples of how to change "You" into "I". Next time you have to give some feedback, particularly negative, write out your feedback as an "I message".

Changing "You" into "I"

"You" message ...	"I" message ...
You never do anything that I want correctly.	*I would like to see the process done this way.*
Why can't you do what I tell you?	*I'd like my instructions followed.*
Your performance is not up to standard.	*I'm disappointed that the performance standards we agreed are not being met.*
You always make that mistake.	*It's disappointing to me that this mistake occurs regularly. I'd like to see the procedures routinely followed.*
You should not push so hard. It's rude and it gets everyone upset.	*I get upset when I see the client flinch sometimes during meetings. My impressions are that they react negatively to the use of some of your words and phrases.*
You have not met one of the key objectives we set at the start of the period.	*I'm disappointed that all of the key objectives that we set at the start of the period have been missed.*
You made a mistake.	*That's incorrect. I'd like to see it done this way.*
You should have called earlier.	*I'd like to get a call in plenty of time to meet the deadline.*
Why didn't you call us when you found out about the changes?	*I would like to hear about this sooner so that I can address the changes in plenty of time.*
You have to fill out these forms.	*I need to have these forms completed.*
Your report was not handed in on time last week which made me look very stupid in the meeting.	*I was disappointed that I did not get your report on time. This made it very hard for me during the meeting.*

Rule 4: Criticise and praise the act, not the person

When we criticise the person (which often happens every time we use the "you" word to describe past behaviour), we are in fact attacking their self esteem, their identity. People can accept the fact that they make mistakes from time to time. They cannot accept that they are a bad person. As has been said many times; "Be hard on the act, not the person."

For example, far better to say "<u>I'm</u> disappointed with the way that transaction was handled" rather than "<u>You</u> are not handling those transactions at all well".

As with all six rules, this one also applies when giving positive feedback. When giving positive feedback, it's obviously not personal criticism that the person is likely to feel, rather possible embarrassment the person may suffer.

For example it's rather hard not to feel a little uneasy when a manager says to us "I really like you". However, we feel great when the boss says something like "I really like the way that report was put together last week. Well done, it was a great job! Keep up the good work."

Rule 4, "Criticise and praise the act" is a prerequisite to rules 5 & 6 because it forces you to be very clear about the behaviour you are either criticising or praising.

Rule 5: Give examples of behaviour and why it is causing you pain or pleasing you

Be very specific. The person needs to know what they have done that is not up to or exceeds your expectations and most importantly, why.

For example; *"I was disappointed that I did not get your report on time. This made it very hard for me during the meeting."*

Telling people "why" gives them the logic behind your feedback. This is just as important when giving positive feedback.

Rule 6: Reinforce "best" behaviour

Let the person know when they have met or exceeded your standards and when they have not. Now, you could say that this is similar to, or in fact part of Rule 5. And you'd be right! The reason it is a separate rule is that not only is it important when giving feedback, but it must become a state of mind. If your people are to become truly good at what they do and most importantly, for you to become a truly great manager, you must constantly look to reinforce best behaviour.

Mentioned elsewhere in this book is the importance of recognition. In countless studies, employees rank "recognition" as the number one motivating factor for them. Reinforcing and recognising best behaviour is the simplest and most effective feedback tool you have – please use it often.

Why we sometimes get it wrong!

Feedback is such an important part of the manager's role, included below are some of the mistakes managers often make with "feedback" so that you can avoid these. I'm indebted to Judith Lindenberger for reminding me of many of these points in her great article "Truth or Consequence? How to give employee feedback". Here's the common mistakes Judith identified:

Some tips for giving feedback . . .

- **Speaking out only when things are wrong.**

  As Earl Nightingale once said: "Praise to a human being represents what sunlight, water and soil are to a plant - the climate in which one grows best."

- **"Drive-by" praise**

  Without specifics or an honest underpinning. For example, "Great job!" This doesn't tell the person the "what" or "why" it was a great job.

- **Waiting until performance or behavior is substantially below expectations before acting on it.**

  It will not improve with time, nor will your feedback message. Give the feedback as close to the event as possible.

- **Giving positive or negative feedback long after the event has occurred.**

  People will have forgotten what it was all about.

- **Not taking responsibility for your thoughts, feelings and reactions.**

  For example, "This comes straight from the boss." Repeated messages such as this will give your people the impression that you are a messenger rather

---

than their manager.

- **Giving feedback through e-mail / text messages, notes, or over the telephone.**

  This is probably one of the worst mistakes I have seen managers make as the opportunity for meaningful dialogue is taken away.

- **Giving negative feedback in public.**

  This is the ultimate humiliation. It makes you look small as well as the person.

- **Criticising performance without giving suggestions for improvement.**

  How will the person know what they need to do to improve?

- **No follow up afterwards.**

  Without follow up the feedback merely becomes empty words.

- **Not having regularly scheduled performance review meetings.**

Adapted from Lindenberger, J. Truth or Consequence? How To Give Employee Feedback.
http://www.lindenbergergroup.com/art_common.html

HOW TO IMPLEMENT THE IDEAS IN THIS CHAPTER

How to start Giving Feedback straight away

Give positive feedback, often.

- Look for examples of behaviour that are up to or beyond your expectations from each of your employees, NOW!

- Write down the words that you are going to use to describe the behaviour you want to praise.

- Practise what you are going to say, at least the opening few sentences.

- Do not sandwich critical feedback between two positive pieces of feedback. It's an inedible sandwich.

If you have to give some negative feedback: . . .

- As the manager, you must always maintain ownership of the problem.
- The aim of the feedback process is to have the employee take ownership of the solution.
- Always describe the action of the employee, not them, their personality or their character.
- Use positive words and avoid words such as "you", "but", "Yes, but".
- Above all once you have given the message, listen, listen, listen!
- Be prepared to discuss the employee's suggestions for how he/she intends to solve the problem. Often the employee will come up with a better solution than you had first thought of. Most importantly, because it's their suggestion, they will have commitment for its implementation.

Stick to the six rules for giving feedback . . .

1. **Get straight to the point**
2. **Keep good news and bad news separate**
3. **Use "I" messages and avoid using "You"**
4. **Criticise or praise the act, not the person**
5. **Give examples of behaviour and why it is causing you pain or pleasing you**
6. **Reinforce "best" behaviour. Let the person know when they have met or exceeded your standards and when they have not**

☞ How to get the most out of Giving Feedback as a new manager

Steps to take when giving <u>negative</u> feedback . . .	Some examples of the words you might use . . .
Step 1: **As the manager, you must take responsibility for the performance problem.** After all, if the employee's performance does not improve, whose problem is it?	You might start the conversation with :"Andrew, I have an (issue / problem / situation) that I need your help with."
Step 2: **Describe the behaviour that is causing you the problem.** Remember, what is the behaviour that is not up to your expectations?	"For the last three weeks, the reports I get each week from your department have been at least a day late."
Step 3: **Explain why this is a problem for you.** This gives your employee the logic behind the feedback you are giving.	"This means that I can't get the reports collated with those from the other departments in time to get them to the GM to meet his deadline."
Step 4: **Explain the possible consequences for you, the manager.** Once again, this reinforces why your feedback is so important.	"The GM got annoyed with me last week and I'm sure he expects much higher performance from my department. I know that if this continues, he is likely to come down on me pretty hard."
Step 5: **Tell him/her how you feel about the problem.** This explains to your employee why you are feeling the way you are. Together with steps 3 and 4, your employee now knows both your thinking <u>and</u> feeling about how their behaviour is impacting you.	"I am keen to keep a good relationship with our GM as it is very important to the success of our department"
Step 6: **Ask for his/her assistance.** You are now handing the responsibility for solving the problem over to your employee.	"What can you do to help me solve this issue / problem / situation?"

The underlying principles to keep in mind when applying this approach are:

- As the manager, you always maintain **ownership of the problem.**
- The aim of the process is to have the employee take **ownership of the solution**.
- Always describe the action of the employee, not them, their personality or their character.
- Use positive words and avoid words such as "you", "but", "Yes, but".
- Above all, when you get to step 6, listen, listen, listen! Be prepared to discuss the employee's suggestions for how he/she intends to solve the problem.

Steps to take when giving <u>positive</u> feedback . . .	Some examples of the words you might use . . .
Step 1: **Tell the person in specific, descriptive terms the behaviour s/he did correctly or well AND the impact of that behaviour.**	"Jill I really like the great job on the Project X report I asked you to complete last week. I was especially impressed with the analysis of the numbers and the explanation of the statistics in the written part of the report"
Step 2: **Tell the person how you feel about the behaviour or how the behaviour will affect others – be specific.**	"I'm confident the GM will be able to make an informed decision because of the quality of the information provided"
Step 3: **Encourage more of the same behaviour.**	"Thanks for doing such a thorough job. Keep up the good work, particularly your great analytical summaries"

Remember, the six rules for giving feedback apply equally to both positive and negative feedback.

Chapter 8

Coaching: How to help your people to take commitment for their own development

Coaching – a stock tool of trade for the new manager

I recently conducted a coaching session on "How to be an effective coach" for a group of very senior financial service advisors. These people were responsible for the management and leadership of project teams that have clients of the mega rich variety. When I asked them what they thought an ideal coach should be, I expected to get descriptions such as:

- Someone in charge of training an athlete or a sports team
- A person who gives private instruction such as singing or acting
- Someone who gives help and advice to others

This is the traditional view of a coach - someone who advises and shows others how to improve in a particular field.

To my amazement, my group of senior financial advisors came up with quite a different list from what I expected. They suggested an ideal coach is someone who:

- Does not give advice, rather helps the person find out what they should do
- Is a good listener
- Has a calming affect on the person being coached (the "coachee")
- "Lives" with the coachee's issues, i.e. suspends judgment and really gets involved
- Displays a positive attitude toward the coachee

- Is always positive about finding a solution or helping the person develop

- Is proud of the coachee's achievements

- Rarely shows emotions such as anger or annoyance

- Helps the coachee talk things through, particularly when the coachee is depressed

- Has a caring attitude toward the coachee

- Provides the coachee with a "comfort zone" where the person is free to say what he/she thinks and feels

Could I come up with a better list? Probably not. They then proceeded to develop a mission for a coach which they suggested should be:

"Asks questions to help the person find answers"

By this stage as the facilitator, I was feeling quite redundant, but tremendously elated. Their enlightened view of a coach made it very easy for me to introduce them to coaching as a development tool they could use with the people in their project teams. They had expressed the philosophy superbly, all they needed then were the tools and techniques.

Training or Coaching?

As a new manager, coaching should be a key tool of trade for developing your people to their full potential. The underlying principle of contemporary coaching as a development tool for managers, is that it encourages the person being coached to take responsibility for their own development.

This doesn't render traditional training (e.g. imparting skill or knowledge by an expert) as redundant, rather it enhances and enables training to be more focused. Sometimes a training course or process can become part of the coaching solution.

How should you decide on training or coaching?

Here are some general guidelines that can help you decide when to train and / or when to coach.

Training . . .	*Coaching . . .*
• should be used when both you and your employee (or group of employees) **see and agree** that they need to develop or improve a specific area of skill or knowledge	• should be used when **you** as the person's manager **see a skill or knowledge deficit** that the em-**ployee may not see,** which may be **causing you a problem**
• is used to **develop skills and knowledge, not solve problems**	• can also be used when an em-**ployee** or **colleague** approaches you **asking for your help to solve a problem**
• can apply to **one person** or a **group of people** with similar needs	• only applies to **one person at a time**
• is delivered or facilitated by a **subject matter expert**	• is facilitated by **someone skilled in coaching**, not necessarily an expert in the subject matter
• **provides answers** to the trainee's questions	• **asks questions** to help the **person find their own answers**

When is the most appropriate time to Coach?

Because coaching relies on the person being coached to:

- identify that they have a need
- assess and agree how this is affecting their current situation
- take responsibility for implementing a solution

there are certain times when the person requiring development will be more ready or amenable to coaching. Some ideas of when to coach are listed below:

When might your employee be ready for coaching?	Why is coaching appropriate at this time?
• **Immediately after the person has experienced a major failure**	For example, your employee may have missed a major deadline, had a serious customer situation, had a blow-up with a fellow team member and so on
• **Immediately after a major success**	In this case, the person will often be keen to see how this success can be repeated and indeed improved upon
• **At the start of a new job, project or assignment**	Particularly where the person is excited and keen to do well
• **At the end of an old job, project or assignment**	Where it is generally accepted that at least an informal process of evaluation occurs
• **When the person has just received some powerful feedback, which may not have been expected**	This can either be positive or negative - for instance when a senior manager criticises a decision or project activity, or a customer gives some quite public and perhaps unexpected praise for a job well done

The GROW model of coaching

There are a number of different coaching models or techniques in use today. One of the best is the GROW model, first introduced by John Whitmore ("Coaching for Performance: Growing People, Performance and Purpose". Nicholas Brealey Publishing. London. 2002).

The GROW model embodies all the attributes my financial advisors described. The aim of the model is to help the coachee arrive at some resolution to their issue, problem, knowledge or skill deficit, not give them advice or direction on what they should do.

GROW stands for

1. **Goal,**
2. **Reality,**
3. **Options,**
4. **Will (sometimes also referred to as Wrap-up**

1. <u>GOAL</u> to be achieved . . .	2. <u>REALITY</u> to be checked . . .
• **Agree the topic for this discussion** • **Agree specific objectives of this session only** • **Set long term aims if this is appropriate**	• **Help coachee assess the current situation** • **Invite self-assessment** • **Offer specific examples of feedback (if you have them)** • **Avoid or check your own assumptions**
3. <u>WILL</u> (or Wrap Up) . . .	4. <u>OPTIONS</u> to be canvassed . . .
• **Help coachee commit to selected actions** • **Identify possible/potential obstacles** • **Develop strategies for managing obstacles** • **Ensure steps are specificand define timing for each** • **Agree support to be provided**	• **Canvass all possible options for change** • **Encourage suggestions for change from the coachee** • **Offer your own suggestions carefully** • **Help coachee define and refine choices**

Adapted from Whitmore J. "Coaching for Performance: Growing People, Performance and Purpose". Nicholas Brealey Publishing. London. 2002

It is a sequential model, ideally working from Goal through to Will. However in practice, it is often found that coach and coachee will move back and forth between the first three stages as they work through the issue.

Here's the model in overview . . .

The GROW model

Stage 1:   Agree the GOAL to be achieved during this session

You and the coachee need to identify and agree on clear and achievable goals for this particular discussion.

This goal is not the longer-term aim that the coachee might have regarding his or her issue. Rather it is the definition of what can be achieved within the time set for this first discussion session. For example, the coachee may not be very clear at this point about their long term aim. But they do know they have some sort of a deficit in either skill or knowledge. So, the coach might ask "What would you like to achieve from this session?" or "What would you like to walk away with from our discussion today?"   Coaching may involve a number of sessions to achieve the final aim.

Stage 2:   Check the current situation to find REALITY

In this stage, your aim as the coach is to help the coachee clearly define the current situation as seen by both coachee and others. For example you might ask "What's happening now?" or "What's working/what's not working for you at the moment?" or "Who else has seen this or given you feedback?"

If you have knowledge of the situation, you may add your perceptions to assist the coachee to build as accurate a picture of reality as possible.

Stage 3: Canvass as many OPTIONS as possible to achieve the goal

In the options stage, your intention is to draw out all the possible alternatives or options the coachee might have (or be able to acquire) to deal successfully with the situation.

This is done without judgment or evaluation by you – this can be very tough on the coach as it is tempting to jump in with a solution that you can clearly see is the most appropriate. However, as was once said to me by an experienced coach, "You should develop an opinion, not have an opinion". You can do this through effective questioning. Questioning helps the coachee narrow the options to arrive at the best possible alternatives. For example you could ask: "What could you do to change the situation?" or "Do you think there might be any alternatives to that approach?". There are some more sample questions at the end of this chapter.

Stage 4: WRAP-UP the session and make sure the coachee has the WILL to implement the agreed solutions

In this stage your intention is to gain the coachee's commitment or will to take action. You should help the coachee:

- Select the most appropriate option
- Commit to taking action
- Define the action plan, which should include:
  - o the next steps and
  - o a timeframe for when they will be completed
- Identify how to overcome any possible obstacles.

Questions you could ask during the wrap-up; "What are the next steps for you?", "When will this happen?", "What might get in the way?", "How will you ensure these obstacles don't stop you achieving your goal?" and "What support do you need?"

Coaching of this type, can be a fantastic tool for helping someone develop. However, to be successful:

- The coach must have a real and genuine interest in helping the coachee

- The coach must believe that the coachee can improve
- The coachee must be willing to be coached

The challenge as a coach in applying a technique such as the GROW model, is to remain non-directive. You must only ask questions, summarise and listen. You should only give advice when it is asked for and then only during the Options and Will stages. For many of us this is quite a major challenge as our normal directive style is the polar opposite. The payoff in mastering this challenge to become non-directive, is to see the coachee take real ownership for their development knowing that you were the catalyst.

To make sure you are in the right frame of mind before taking on the coach's role it may be useful to ask yourself:

- Do I really want to help this person develop himself/herself?
- Why do I want to do this?

HOW TO IMPLEMENT THE IDEAS IN THIS CHAPTER

☞ How to start Coaching straight away

Practise using the following four questions when you see some of your people struggling with an issue or when they come to you with a problem.

GOAL

*   What are you trying to achieve right now?

REALITY

*   What's happening at the moment that's preventing you from achieving that?

OPTIONS

*   What are the options you can take? Which is the most appropriate?

WILL

*   What will you do now to take this option forward and make it happen?

☞ How to get the most out of Coaching as a new manager

1. Start with issues or problems your people present to you
Once you:

*   have become familiar and comfortable with the four stage GROW model and
*   feel that you understand and can work through the four stages and the basic questions above, try using the approach when some of your people come to you with more in-depth or seemingly complex issues.

2. Move onto issues you identify in others
When you feel you have mastered the approach with issues or problems your people present to you, try using the approach when you see a team member whom you believe has a skill or knowledge deficit, but they don't see it that way.

Some suggested questions for each of the four stages

Take these questions and adapt them to suit your own style. Keep in mind that the questions should be:

- Open and not closed, i.e. they should all start with What, Where, How, Why?

1. GOAL to be achieved in this session	2. REALITY to be checked
• What would you like to get from our discussion? • What would you like to achieve? • What would you like to see happening that's not happening now? • What would you like to see about the situation that is different?	• What's the current situation? • How do you know this? • What feedback have you received? • How often does this happen? • What's the impact? • What have you tried so far?
3. OPTIONS to be canvassed	**4. WILL to carry out the agreed solution**
• What could you do to change the situation? • What are the options that are available to you? • What are the plusses and minuses of these options? • Would you like any suggestions from me? • Which do you think is the most appropriate option to address the issue?	• What will you do now? • What are the next steps? • When will these happen? • What are the likely barriers to your success? • How will you overcome these barriers? • What help would you like from me? • How will you know when you are successful?

Keep in mind that you will most likely move back and forth between stages 1, 2 and 3. As you do, it is important to:

- Stay focused. Your goal is to ensure that the coachee takes ownership and responsibility for the final solution.

- Ensure that you get a conclusion for each of the four stages, i.e.
1. Goal - What exactly is to be achieved in this coaching session?
2. Reality - What is the reality of the situation?
3. Options - What are all the possible solutions? Which is most appropriate?
4. Will - What is the coachee going to do now and when will this happen?
- Above all, keep faith that the coachee has the solutions and the means to the solution, within him or her. Avoid giving your solution even though it may be a good one. Far better to have an employee committed to a positive course of action than perhaps grudgingly compliant to something that their manager suggests.

Chapter 9

How to manage the Appraisal Process

Performance Appraisals – why is there so much anxiety about both doing and receiving them?

Y ou've probably either been the subject of an appraisal or had to give one to someone. Most people find the process uncomfortable, so you aren't alone. There are three reasons for our anxiety with performance appraisals:

1. We are not used to being appraised
2. The person doing the appraising is not well skilled
3. The appraisal process or system being used is poorly designed

Take the case of Derek in the following story, "79.9".

Derek and "79.9"

"Oh, there you are," said the supervisor of Team Four, 4pm to 12am shift, at the FabCola Customer Service Centre. "Don't be shy," he enthused, his smile almost warm. "Have a seat, and make yourself comfortable."

Derek reached for the chair, but it was bolted to the floor. At FabCola, comfort meant fitting in, even with the pre-arranged furniture.

The supervisor continued with his patter. "So – " (he thumbed through the papers in front of him) "Derek? – how are you faring at Customer Service Station 117?"

"Ah, everything's fine, Sir." Derek's eyes dropped back to his lap. They would have stayed there, too, but the supervisor began tapping at the performance reports.

"Well, let's see before we make any snap judgements, eh?" A smile, five degrees above freezing. The supervisor scanned the wad of papers before him. Charts, histograms, tables, and percentages. "Mm. Not too bad at all, actually. Would you like to know your average score? Of course you would. You wouldn't be here otherwise."

With a practised start, Derek sat straight in his chair, at a calculated angle of keenness inclined twenty five degrees away from vertical towards the supervisor. Earlier that day, a scrap of paper had been slid into his 1.0 by 1.5 metre cubicle: the informal office grapevine – what was left of it – had told Derek how to answer this question. With a fixed expression of eagerness glazing over his features, he almost shouted, "Yes, sir! I would love to know my average score. And I would welcome any suggestions for my continued development that you might share with me!"

The supervisor beamed. That was more like it! "Now, before we get too excited," (the high beam began to dim) "I should remind you that bonus points only accrue from scores of 80 or more. Your average is 79.9" (Bonus points were a currency unto themselves at FabCola, and could be used to secure subsidised electricity, computer and 'phone rental for the cubicle, or, with scores of 95 or more, life's little luxuries, like stationary, or a chair with a backrest. Without bonus points, the take-home pay didn't stretch very far...) "Your use of company lingo has improved to 88%, and you've taken ownership of 94% of customer problems brought before you. That's the good news." Derek flinched in anticipation of what was to come. "But, and that's a big but," the supervisor emphasised, "your rest-break efficiency is only 70%, and your creativity quotient only 67.6%. See here – you're taking two minutes to complete a number one. Now multiply that by your running average of two-a-day, and we have a real problem. Something wrong with your bladder?"

Derek began to sweat. "Sir, what if I was to cut down on my liquids during the day – "

"Need I remind you that FabCola is a business, not a charity? How will you get through the mandatory twelve cans a day with that hair-brained scheme? I expect better from you at the next review."

Derek's third performance review was over. One more, and he could call it a day. All in all, he had to admit that it wasn't a bad first day.

Shaun Saunders 'Navigating In The New World', Shaun A. Saunders, 2007

Hopefully you've not had an experience like Shaun Saunders' Derek . Unfortunately, behind Shaun's tongue in cheek look at the world of appraisals, there may be one or two things that get a little too close to the truth.

Let's start at the beginning . . .

Why do organisations have appraisals?

Appraisals were first introduced to ensure that those managers or supervisors who did not intuitively give their employees adequate, regular and timely feedback, were forced to do so.

In fact the very first formal appraisal processes were introduced in factories during the industrial revolution in Britain in the 1800s. They consisted of small wooden blocks suspended over the work station of each employee. The blocks were attached to a string that the supervisor could use to turn the face of the block. Depending on the employee's level of performance, on each face was a different word, such as "Good", "Poor", "Satisfactory" and "Excellent". Talk about "immediate feedback"!

You might say that their method was rather draconian. At least it was feedback and it was instant. These are often the two things that many modern managers miss out on – giving people both positive and negative feedback at the time of the performance. Compare this to your relationship with your spouse or partner. How would you feel if they only told you they loved you once a year? It's also similar with negative feedback in your personal relationships. Most marriages and partnerships start to break up because of the lack of feedback on the little things that regularly annoy each party – there is often agreement on jointly held values or major issues because they were the values that started the partnership. However, it's the little, regular, annoying things that cause the split to occur.

Modern organisations initially introduced the annual appraisal process to cover for the omissions of their managers in giving regular feedback. It seems as though nothing has changed much since their first introduction - in a recent Human Resources Forum poll, 56% of respondents said that the only feedback they received during the year was at annual appraisal time.

Few issues in management stir up more controversy than performance appraisal. If every manager did his or her job as a manager and gave feedback regularly and naturally, we would not have the need for the appraisal system that causes both manager and employee so much anxiety. It would be nice if both employees and managers could say that they find the appraisal process easy, comfortable and enjoyable.

Over the last 30 years or so, the appraisal process has been expanded to not only include feedback on performance, but to link it to salary and career development. It is now often referred to as the "Performance Management System".

How can you improve the process?

Bob's R20

When I first started work as a young bank clerk, I had a work buddy Michael, who was assigned to look after me. Michael had already been in the organisation a year, so he was an expert (a fact that he often reminded me of). After a few months at the bank, Michael said to me one day "Bob, you'll get your R20 done soon". At first I thought it was something I had forgotten to do, or perhaps the R20 was another one of the many bank forms or returns I had to complete.

Apparently, my R20 was my annual performance appraisal form that was completed by my manager. It was also done without the need or requirement by the bank, to discuss it with me. The R20 was then sent off to Head Office as a key input to my future career prospects. For a number of years, I never saw my R20.

Some years later, I started working for Kendall Smith in another department of the bank. Like my first manager, Kendall too had to complete my R20. The major difference was the different approach that Kendall took with the same R20. Here's how Kendall handled the appraisal process:

1. *For starters, he gave me regular feedback on my performance throughout the year as it happened.*

2. *Then, every quarter he completed the R20 in pencil. (the bank only required the form to be completed annually).*

3. *Each quarter, he gave me a copy of the R20 and said "Bob, if this were the annual R20, this is what it would contain. I'd like you to have a look at it, then come back to me in a couple of days time and we will spend an hour or so discussing both our thoughts." (the bank at this time still did not require managers to discuss the annual appraisal with the employee).*

4. *When the annual appraisal date came around, there were no surprises and I virtually knew what my R20 would contain before Kendall handed it to me for comment.*

Kendall did this for every one of his 26 team members. No wonder it was such a great place to work and he was such a good manager. In fact, I developed more in the three years that I worked for him than I had ever done previously.

A sample quarterly review

If you do not have a formal quarterly review process or you are interested in implementing this approach, here's a very easy way to do it.

Each quarter, complete the following review form. Also ask your team member to do the same. Then, get together and discuss results. (Of course you can add other Performance Areas to this form or change it to match with your formal organisational review process – it's the principle that's important)

Performance Area	Doing well	Needs some improvement	Requires significant improvement
Quality of work			
Quantity of work			
Timeliness of results			
Stakeholder relationships			
Problem solving			
Application of technical knowledge and skills			
Application of people skills			
	↑	↑	↑
Action required by manager ➜	*Recognise and praise good performance*	*Undertake coaching in required areas*	*Complete a written development plan (3 mths)*

Frequent feedback – more is better

If you feel that giving feedback is one of the things you need to do more of, you can provide feedback more regularly. I spoke with one manager recently who has six people reporting to him. Every week he sits down and has a half-hour session with one of his six reports and provides them with feedback. So, his people get a semi-formal feedback session once every six weeks. He told me that since he has started this process, the improvement in the relationship between he and his team has increased dramatically. Not only that, but there is now much more openness within the team and they have started to give one another feedback.

The appraisal process – what to do when you have to appraise the performance of a team member

As with my experience with Kendall, when you are managing your people, there should be no surprises at annual appraisal time. Here are some suggestions to help make the process a positive one for both you and your team member:

1. At the start of the appraisal period, usually 12 months, set and agree your performance standards with each of your team members (Performance Standards are covered in Chapter 5).
2. Provide your team members with regular feedback (both positive and negative) throughout the year on their performance, as it happens (Giving Feedback is covered in Chapter 7).
3. Complete a mini review at various times during the year. If you can manage it, quarterly is good.
4. At appraisal time, ask your team member to review their objectives that had been set and agreed 12 months ago. Get them to list:
    *   Performance that has been up to or beyond expectations, and
    *   Areas of performance that require further development.
5. Independently. complete this same exercise on your team member's performance yourself.
6. Conduct your appraisal discussion using the lists you and your team member prepared. Discuss and reach agreement on each area of performance.

What about when I am being appraised?

There are two sides to the appraisal process. If you are on the receiving side it is worthwhile thinking through beforehand how you can make it a positive experience for yourself.

This is the time when you will feel the apprehension of being appraised by your boss. Let's hope it's a far more positive experience that poor Derek had with his 79.9 average.

How can you manage the situation to gain maximum benefit?

Perhaps your boss is like my manager Kendall. If, so then you will not need to read any further. Just go for it!

If your boss is not so good at doing the appraisals of his or her people, here are some tips that may help improve the experience for you:

1. Give your boss a copy of this chapter. Better still, give him or her a copy of the book – it may dramatically improve your boss' entire performance!
2. At appraisal time, review your objectives and list:
    *   Performance that has been up to or beyond expectations, and
    *   Areas of performance that require further development

    This will give you some really good evidence to call on during the meeting
3. Review the main priorities your boss has in his or her own role (Chapter 12 "How to Manage Your Boss" covers these). What have you done to assist your boss in these? Make sure you have some good examples.
4. Whenever there is disagreement over particular points, always ask for examples of your behaviour that will clarify it for you.

Whether you are appraising the performance of one of your team, or your performance is being appraised by your boss, the important thing to keep in mind is that appraisal is about performance, not personality.

HOW TO IMPLEMENT THE IDEAS IN THIS CHAPTER

☛ How to start appraising straight away

As performance appraisal in most organisations is an annual event, there are only a couple of things you can do immediately.

1. Make sure you have set and agreed performance standards with each team member at the start of the appraisal period. If not, undertake this now.

2. Arrange to do mini reviews during the year.
3. Look to give people feedback regularly on their performance as it happens.

☞ How to become an expert at performance appraisals

When conducting appraisals for your people:

1. Go to Chapter 7 "How to give Feedback – Positive and Negative" and read it thoroughly. It will provide you with some very good tips not only on giving feedback, but what to say and do in the appraisal interview.

2. Make sure you have set and agreed performance standards with each team member at the start of the appraisal period. If not, undertake this now. This is covered in Chapter 5 "How to set Performance Standards for your people".

3. Arrange to do mini reviews every quarter.

4. Look to give people feedback regularly on their performance as it happens.

When having your own performance appraised:

1. Review your objectives and list:
   - Performance that has been up to or beyond expectations, and
   - Areas of performance that require further development

2. Review the main priorities your boss has in his or her role (Chapter 12 "How to Manage Your Boss"). What have you done to assist your boss in these? Make sure you have some good examples.

3. Whenever there is disagreement over particular points, always ask for examples of your behaviour that will clarify it for you.

Chapter 10

If you have to, How to Fire Someone

Inspiration to write this chapter came about through the recent experience of two of my friends. Both had been fired. One for supposed poor performance, although she had never been counselled and at the time was in fact on sick leave and one because the start up facility she was employed by, suddenly closed down. Both were senior managers. Both were loyal, hardworking employees but are now very angry and taking legal action against their former employers.

Why are they so angry?

One could say it's because they have lost their jobs and this would be quite understandable. However, the main action that has triggered their anger and catapulted them down the legal pathway (in both cases), was that they were informed of their dismissals by emails. Yes, that's right by email! They were never given the courtesy of a face to face discussion.

What emotions does the other person experience?

Many managers, when faced with the challenge of firing someone, forget, or are unaware of the emotions that are experienced by the person being fired. Nor are they aware of the behaviour that most often results from these emotions.

It has been well documented that the death of a loved one, a marriage or long term relationship break-up and the loss of one's job, have an equal and similar impact on one's emotions. Think for a moment about the loss of one of your dear relatives or friends through death – how did you feel? That's exactly the same feeling that people have when they suddenly and unexpectedly lose their jobs.

The Five Stages of Grief

The psychologists tell us that there are five stages that people go through in what they call a "grief cycle" –

1. **Shock**
2. **Resistance**, which is often manifested as anger
3. **Acceptance** of the current situation
4. **Exploration** of new opportunities
5. **Commitment** to a new future

Following is how the Grief Cycle looks as a flow process moving from Shock through all five stages to Commitment.

The Grief Cycle

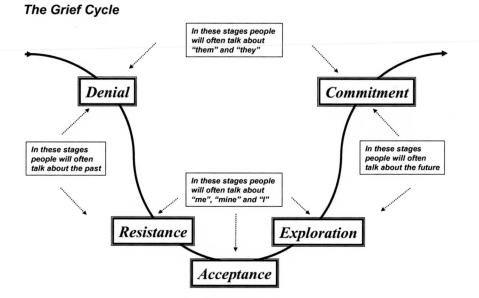

Can any of these emotions be managed via email?

The experience of firing someone . . .

I can well recall the first time as a manager I had to fire someone. It was for poor performance and I was scared. I did not sleep the night before wondering what I would say and what would be her reaction. I carried out the interview in the morning with great fear and trepidation. I was not sure how the interview went, but was relieved when it was over. I then took a break for lunch, but was unable to eat. I did not know about the "five stages" at the time, I only knew that I had to do the right thing by the organisation and by the employee.

I arrived back from my break to find a box of chocolates on my desk with a very nice note from the employee saying how much she appreciated my courtesy and kindness. I guess, intuitively I must have got something right.

Now, from years of experience, I know two things about firing someone:

- Firstly, the person at all times must maintain his or her self esteem. This is one of the most basic and important needs that all people have. Emailing someone, or even worse as I heard since starting this chapter, texting, sends a clear message that they are not worthy of a face to face discussion.

- Secondly, it is vitally important to realise that all people will go through the five stages of the grief cycle, but quite often at different paces. As a manager, it is your role to help them progress through these stages. This is particularly true for the first two stages that the person is likely to experience when they are still with you. The chances are very high that the person being fired will feel 'Shock' at the point in the interview when you announce the firing and will exhibit 'Resistance' before the interview is over. Will you be prepared to help the person through these stages?

Things to consider when firing someone

How do you do this? Well, in my usual style when writing a chapter such as this, I did my web research. Sad to say there was not much there. Under "firing someone" there seems to be a plethora of articles about the legal requirements and many about the steps to take. For example, one article suggested the following steps:

- Give warning
- Document, Document, Document!

- Time it right
- Prepare the paperwork
- Don't go it alone (ensure you have someone from HR there),
- Ensure privacy
- Be brief
- Watch your tone
- Seek feedback
- Give a good send-off.

How many of these steps would address the five stages of grief? I think, not many. In fact, many of these could probably be done by email with the same impact and result. If these steps were followed, I wonder what "feedback" the manager would receive – would there be a "Good send-off"?

It's not suggested that you don't have to address some of these. For example, you must cover all of the documentary and legal responsibilities pertinent to your country and organisation's requirements. But keep in mind that the fired employee is first and foremost a person just like you with feelings and emotions just like you, that must be managed. It's getting the management of the emotions right that will set you apart as an effective manager, not crossing all the "t"s and dotting all the "i"s, important as some of them may be.

What's the impact on those who stay?

One factor that is often overlooked when firing someone, is that the way it is done can have as much impact (positive or negative) on the people who remain. They will be watching and will invariably get a first hand report from their colleague, about how well or otherwise the process was managed.

Even when (as often happens) others say "The boss should have got rid of that person months ago" they will still want to know that the firing was done sympathetically.

The people who remain in the organisation, and whom I assume you want to keep, get a good look at both yours and the organisation's real people management skills when under the stress of firing someone.

They'll most certainly ask "Could this happen to me?"

HOW TO IMPLEMENT THE IDEAS IN THIS CHAPTER

When next you have to fire someone

The following suggestions, assume that you have fulfilled all the other documentary and legal requirements.

Things to consider ...	Things to do ...
1. Before taking any action, ask yourself: "How would I feel if my boss came to me today and said – you're fired!"	• Write down a list of words that describe your **feelings if you were being fired**
2. If you were in the situation of being fired, how would you like your boss to handle it? What would you like him/her to do and to say?	• Jot down some of your thoughts – i.e. **the way you would like to be treated** and what you would like **your boss to say to you**
3. Consider both your own feelings about firing someone as well as how they might be feeling	• Now write down a list of the words that best describe your feelings about having to fire someone • Review all the words you have scribbled down so far and pick out the two or three strongest • Also keep in mind how you would like to be handled in similar circumstances
4. Script the start of the conversation using the two or three words you have discovered	• e.g. "This is really difficult for me. I feel apprehensive and worried that I won't get it right" Or, you could say; "I've got some bad news ....."
5. The next part of your opening script will depend on the circumstances – think about these before the interview	• e.g. In "lay off" situation, it might go something like; "I have been advised that I have to terminate the employment of a number of people. I am really sad

	to say that your name is on that list"
	• Or, for a non performance issue, it could be something like; "We have discussed my expectations about your performance and unfortunately they are still not being met. It now really saddens me (or whatever your feelings are) that I will have to terminate your employment"
6. Be careful. You can only script the opening few lines, but they are important because they set the scene for the entire interview	• It is most likely that during the remainder of the interview, the employee will travel back and forth between "shock" and "resistance"
	• Give your reasons for the termination clearly and succinctly. These are non-negotiable
	• Do not get into a discussion about justifying yours (or your employer's) reasons. Doing so will keep the employee fixed in either of the first two stages and will not help them to progress
	• Only sincere listening and clear questioning (not reasoning) will help the employee progress to the acceptance stage

Part 3: Managing Upwards and Sideways

How do you get things done when you have no formal control?

In terms of personal power and the ability to influence others, it has been suggested that "you are who you know". This has never been truer than today. In prior times, power came through people's roles – i.e. positional power. In today's organisations that have flatter structures and are often matrix in design, role power is diminishing. Things now more often get done through who you know, not what role you hold. Power rests with the individual, not the role. More and more, it's your ability to get things done through people over whom you have no formal authority - for example, your manager, peers, colleagues, customers, suppliers and so on - that stamps you as an effective manager.

The aim of Part 3, is to provide you with an introduction to some of the really important influencing skills and techniques that are required of an effective manager. For example, in Chapter 11 "How to influence others" I've covered one of the best skill sets that I have ever come across. I've now been applying these skills successfully for the last 20 years and believe they are a major reason for my success, firstly as a manager and more recently, a consultant.

Chapter 11 also has a section on building your network (both internal and external).

Chapter 12 "How to manage your boss" covers one of the defining relationships in your new role – you should read this chapter. The final chapter, 13, is one that I trust you will not need immediately, "How to select your new boss".

Learning tips to help you get the most out of Part 3 . . .

Activists:

- Read the short case study in the first two pages of Chapter 11 on Maureen and Andrea.
- Get a colleague to also read the case study. Meet with your colleague and discuss why Andrea may have been more successful than Maureen.

- Discuss the Influencing Behaviour Model with your colleague – who applied it better?
- Undertake the "How to start influencing straight away" activity at the end of Chapter 11.
- In the exercise at the end of Chapter 12 "How to Manage Your Boss" pick out and apply the one activity that will have most impact with your relationship with him/her.

Pragmatists:

- Go straight to the Influencing Behaviour Model. What do you think your preferred style is?
- Read the section on the Influencing Behaviour Model.

- Ask a colleague to sit in on one of your team meetings and give you some feedback on which influencing style he/she saw you use most.
- Undertake the "How to start influencing straight away" activity at the end of Chapter 11.
- If your relationship with your boss is not as good as it could be, complete the exercise at the end of Chapter 12.

Theorists

- Read Chapter 11 in its entirety. Complete "How to become an expert influencer".
- Ask a trusted colleague to give you some feedback on how appropriately you apply the "feeling" type behaviours described in the chapter.

- Read Chapter 12 "How to Manage Your Boss" and complete the exercise at the end of the chapter.

Reflectors:

- Read Chapter 11 in its entirety. Complete "How to become an expert influencer".
- At the next three meetings you attend, try to identify the behaviours being used by others. After the meeting, re-read the section in Chapter 11 on influencing styles.
- Read Chapter 12 in its entirety. Think about whether you should complete the exercise at the end of the chapter.

Chapter 11

How to Influence Others

What is influencing?

More and more, it's your ability to get things done through people over whom you have no formal authority, for example, your manager, peers, colleagues, customers, suppliers and so on, that stamps you as a good manager. There are also very many people who are in specialist positions – 'sideline people' – who have no authority to tell anybody what to do, but who have a lot of influence because they are perceived to be expert in their field.

There are at least two factors that impact your ability to influence others:

- The **behaviours** you use when interacting with others
- The **influencing strategies** you adopt

Mel Silberman, tells the influencing story of two managers, Maureen and Andrea that demonstrates both of these factors at work.

The case of Maureen and Andrea ...

Maureen, a vice-president of a financial services company, is one of the brightest people I've ever met. And one of the best read and best informed as well. She can be interesting to listen to ...until the point when she wants you to agree with her. If you see things differently, she barrels ahead, stating with complete certainty how right she is. She does provide facts and figures to support what she's saying, but if you still have misgivings, her posture is that "you simply don't understand." Maureen also has little patience when others express views that she disagrees with. You seldom get the impression that she considers what you think or feel. The net result is that she rarely influences the views of others. She may be admired for her brilliance but people keep at arm's length from her. Sensing the rejection of others, Maureen retreats until the next moment she is intent on changing people's minds. Her efforts are always short-lived and unsuccessful.

Compare Maureen to Andrea. Andrea is the training manager in the same financial services company. She recently convinced her company to increase their commitment to training by $2 million dollars annually. This was accomplished by a painstaking personal campaign that lasted two years. When Andrea first suggested to senior management that a greater investment in training its workforce was essential, she was soundly rebuffed with the explanation: "In our experience, training is usually a waste of time and money. People will learn what they really need to on their own or by getting help from their coworkers and supervisors." Although disappointed by this response, Andrea was determined to do whatever it took to influence a change in thinking.

The first thing she did was to talk with senior management about their personal experiences with training when they were first entering the company. She probed into many areas and listened with interest and understanding to the answers she obtained. It was not difficult for her to identify with the negative training experiences people had because she, too, had similar ones. She also asked senior management to share with her the business results they were seeking for the coming two years. Armed with this information, she put together a powerful presentation that featured newer, more effective training strategies. She also suggested how they could be utilized to impact the company's bottom line. Andrea was careful to benchmark the best training practices of other similar companies and establish their "return on investment." This time, Andrea received a better response. Although no commitments were made, she did receive a promise to review her proposal after the next quarter's results.

To make a long story short, the proposal was kicked about for several months before given serious consideration. During that time, Andrea occupied herself with other projects, but also made a point of periodically checking in with her supervisor on the status of her proposal. After a year went by, senior management was becoming convinced of the merits of Andrea's views but still did not commit as much money as she had been seeking. Andrea graciously accepted the small "foot in the door"

148

and, with the budget she had to work with, conducted some pilot pro-
grams that were well received and backed up by data to support their re-
sults. Now, finally convinced of training's effectiveness, senior manage-
ment gave Andrea the total backing she had long been seeking.

"Influencing Others the People-Smart Way" (#567 Innovative Leader
Volume 11, Number 12, December 2002), Mel Silberman

What's happening in these two scenarios?

Maureen appears to be working purely with her natural and instinctive
style, whilst Andrea adopts a much more holistic, strategic and considered approach.

What's involved in such a holistic approach to influencing?

Two factors impact our ability to influence others:

- The **behaviours** we use when face-to-face with others - Did you notice the particular behaviours Maureen and Andrea used, and their
  impact?
- The **influencing strategies** we apply, both short and long term - Andrea was the only one who had both short and long term strategies.
  Maureen relied purely on behaviour with no strategy.

1. The behaviours you use when interacting with others

In addition to using your natural personality to its best advantage, there is
also the behaviour – the actual words and phrases – that impact your
ability to influence others. This behaviour is independent of personality.

You can improve your ability to influence others by being more aware of
the influencing skills you already have in your armory. You just need to
use them more appropriately, **according to the situation.** This last point
needs to be stressed – there are influencing skills that work better in
some situations rather than others.

Step 1: Identify the TYPE of situation	Is the situation ...
	→ *Feeling?*
	or
	→ *Fact?*

So, the first step to applying your influencing skills more productively, is to:

- recognise the **type of situation** you are facing.

Is the person (or people) you are trying to influence at all emotional about the topic? For example;

- Are they worried or excited, sad or happy?

Additionally, what are your feelings about the topic? For instance;

- Do you have some basic inner needs that you must satisfy?

If either you or your influence target are at all emotional about the topic, then you are dealing with a *feeling* type situation.

On the other hand, if both parties see the topic or discussion as factual – i.e. logic and reason prevail over emotion, then you are in a *fact* situation.

Step one is to decide *"Is this situation feeling or fact?"*

As you might now expect, *Feeling* and *Fact* situations require the use of quite different influencing skills.

For example, let's say you're a parent. You want to get your seven year old child to tidy their room. All the reason and logic in the world will not get the child to tidy their room if they don't want to (no doubt many of you can relate to this!). Despite what some of the parental guide books might suggest, experience shows that you need to take a more assertive (*feeling*) type approach rather than a reasoning (*fact*) approach in such a situation.

However the assertive approach taken with your child when they did not want to tidy their room, will probably not work when you want your boss to approve a new item of budget expenditure. In fact it may even work in reverse and get your budget (or you) cut!

Step 2: For FEELING situations	Apply either ...
	➔ *Reflecting* behaviour
	or
	➔ *Asserting* behaviour

How do you manage the *Feeling* situations?

There are two quite different feeling type skills that you could use. For example, when a person comes to you with a personal problem, you will need to apply your reflective listening skills. Whereas, when you have a very strong desire to get your needs met, for instance in a tough negotiating situation, you may need to apply assertive skills.

Whilst these situations are quite different in their context, both are *feeling* type situations – the first is dealing with their feelings, the second is dealing with your feelings. Because of this, each *feeling* influence situation is successfully handled by using different influencing skills.

For **feeling situations**, the most powerful influencing skills are:	
• **Reflecting** . . .	The ability to really *listen* to the underlying message being expressed by *the other* person - not what they may be saying, but what they are really feeling.
• **Asserting** . . .	*Stating your own* needs and expectations strongly.

Fact situations on the other hand, require the skills of questioning and suggesting.

Step 3: For FACT situations	Apply either ...
	➔ *Questioning* behaviour
	or
	➔ *Suggesting* behaviour

Whenever you ask open, non-threatening questions you are using the influencing skill of gathering data. e.g. "I'd like to hear more about your proposal. What are the main reasons why you have suggested this?"

On the other hand, whenever you put forward a proposal, recommendation or merely a suggestion, you are using the influencing skill of suggesting. And your suggestions can become even more powerful when they are supported with strong reasoning. e.g. "There is only one system on the market that meets these requirements (reason) and that is why I recommend the P680 (proposal)".

For **fact situations**, the most powerful influencing skills are:	
• **Questioning** . . .	Ask fact-finding, ***non-judgmental questions*** to gather data and information from the ***other person.***
• **Suggesting** . . .	Make ***proposals*** and ***suggestions*** supported by two or three ***strong reasons*** of what ***you want.***

Employing your natural influencing skills more productively on a daily basis means:

- Deciding whether the situation calls for feeling or fact type influencing skills
- Using the most appropriate feeling or fact influencing skills for the situation.

That sounds all nice and logical. However, we all have natural preferences for using one or more of the various influencing behaviours of Reflecting, Asserting, Questioning and Suggesting. These four behaviours work best in different types of situations. What happens when we tend to continually overuse one of these skills (perhaps because we are very comfortable or experienced with it)? Or, we use one of our preferred influencing skills in an inappropriate situation?

Read Maureen's case again.

- What behaviours do you think she prefers to use more than others?

You can probably see that she is very good at Suggesting and Asserting, but not so good at Questioning and Listening.

Here are some of the times Maureen used Suggesting and Asserting

Maureen was *SUGGESTING* (describing her reason and logic) when ...	Maureen was *ASSERTING* (describing her feelings) when ...
She can be interesting to listen to ...	*... until the point when she wants you to agree with her. If you see things differently, she barrels ahead, stating with complete certainty how right she is*
She does provide facts and figures to support what she's saying ...	*... but if you still have misgivings, her posture is that "you simply don't understand."*
	Maureen also has little patience when others express views that she disagrees with.
	You seldom get the impression that she considers what you think or feel.

If you now read Andrea's case, you will see that she successfully combined all four behaviours at various stages of her campaign to great effect.

Here's a summary of how Andrea used the four behaviours:

QUESTIONING She used reason and logic - theirs	REFLECTING She used feelings - theirs	ASSERTING She used feelings - hers	SUGGESTING She used reason and logic - hers
The first thing she did was to talk with senior management about their personal experiences with training when they were first entering the company	*She probed into many areas and listened with interest and understanding to the answers she obtained.*	*It was not difficult for her to identify with the negative training experiences people had because she, too, had similar ones.*	*She put together a powerful presentation that featured newer, more effective training strategies. She also suggested how they could be utilized to impact the company's bottom line ... to benchmark the best training practices of other similar companies and establish their "return on investment."*
↑ Called "OPENERS" - used at the start of the conversations to open up discussion ↑		↑ Called "CLOSERS" - used later in the conversation to close off discussion ↑	

A model for applying the four behaviours of - Reflecting, Asserting, Questioning and Suggesting

As a general guide:

- **Reflecting** and **Questioning** should be used early in an influencing situation to open up the communication and to gather input about **feelings** and **facts**
- **Asserting** and **Suggesting** should be used later in the influencing situation to present **your needs or feelings** and to **make proposals or suggestions**

The following model provides an overview of how these behaviours might be applied.

INFLUENCING
BEHAVIOUR MODEL

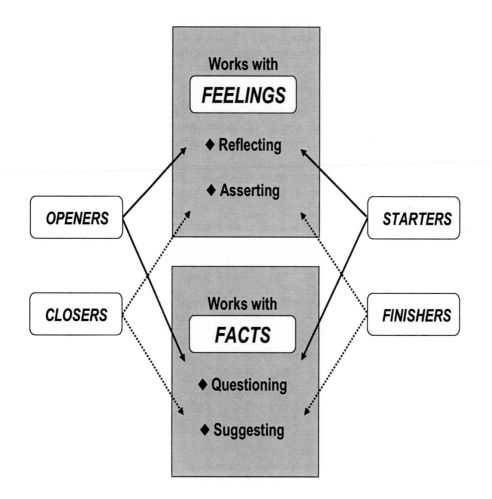

So, next time you want to influence that important person or people, rather than barging in, step back a little and think:

- Is this **fact** or **feeling**?
- What **behaviours** will be most appropriate?
- How do I **combine these**?

2. The influencing strategies you adopt

As well as behaviour, there are also the strategies that you adopt or should adopt, to influence various people and situations.

Short or long term influencing strategies?

These strategies may be very specific and designed or developed for one particular situation, or they may be more broad and designed to build your image as an influencer across the organisation.

How successful your short term strategies are, will be linked very closely to the behaviours you use when discussing them with others.

For example, in Andrea's case, after her initial proposal was rejected, she developed a new strategy for getting her proposal approved that included:

- Talking with senior managers to find out their experiences, particularly negative, they may have had with training programs
- Finding out from senior managers the business results they were seeking for the next two years
- Making a new proposal that featured newer, more effective training strategies
- Suggesting how training could be utilized to impact the company's bottom line
- Benchmarking the best training practices of other similar companies and establishing their return on investment

And when her new proposal was only partially accepted, she adapted her strategy by:

- Periodically checking in with her supervisor on the status of her proposal, then,
- Conducting some pilot programs that were well received and backed up by data to support their results.

Short term influencing strategies – look for the "holes"

So, if you have a particular situation where you need to influence the outcome, it is crucial to develop strategies specifically for that situation. A good technique for doing this is to ask yourself two questions::

1. If my proposal were to be rejected, what could be some of the possible reasons? and,
2. What do I need to do to counter these reasons?

You can also:

- Ask some trusted colleagues for their input to these two questions – What would they do in your situation?
- Ask one or two of the people whom you believe will be most opposed to your proposal to "knock some holes in it for me please, before I put it up for approval". You will be amazed at the information you will get and quite probably the support these people will give, when you do eventually put forward your proposal, which of course, now includes their suggestions.

Remember to use the "opening" up type behaviours of questioning and reflecting to ensure that you get the full range of their opinions and feelings about your proposal.

Armed with this new information, you can now develop a sound proposal that is more likely to be accepted.

Long term influencing strategies – build and maintain your network

Your long term strategies will depend on how well you develop your networks within the organisation. It has been said that "You are who you know". In other words, your influencing power is really enhanced when you have a wide network of people, not only within the organisation, but also outside. You should be able to call on these people when you need help, guidance or advice. And because of your relationship with this network of people, when asked, they will most likely respond positively to your request.

In prior times, power came through people's roles – i.e. positional power. However more and more in today's organisation that is flatter and often matrix, role power is disappearing. Things now get done through who you know, not what role you hold. Power rests with the individual, not the role. So there is both more pressure and more incentive to develop a good network.

What is a network?

Bob's Case

When I first started consulting, one of my business partners said to me "Bob, you know so many people in the industry and you are known to so many people, your people resources are so valuable to our business." I hadn't thought of it that way before. I'd merely been interested in making as many contacts as I possibly could so that I could build my knowledge of the industry and at the same time, help others.

Apparently, what I had been unconsciously doing was building my network. Now, when I think of that experience, I can recall the countless times that these contacts asked for my advice, which I gave very freely. The really great thing about my network was that whenever my boss or another senior manager had a difficult or challenging question that related to our industry or profession, I was able to come up with an answer. It was merely a case of getting on the phone to one of my contacts.

And of course, when I started consulting, my network was invaluable in introducing me to potential clients because they could recommend both my expertise and integrity.

A network could be described as a "series of mutually beneficial relationships." It's a bit like building a community. People who are interested in similar things, join together.

The four rules for building and maintaining your network

- Rule 1: Build volume and diversity in your network
- Rule 2: Give, give, give!
- Rule 3: Make contact with your potential network members
- Rule 4: Keep in touch to maintain your network

Rule 1: Build volume and diversity in your network

Although my original network was good, I realise now that it could have been much better had I developed a lot more contacts rather than focusing only on people who had the same interests as me. Whilst my network that I had developed when working as an employee was useful, as a consultant it needed to be much broader.

As we all do initially, I networked for friendship. It's natural to start building your network with people who are similar to you in personality, style, career and personal interests. However, the people who have the best networks also have the most diverse networks. Add those people who are different to you in personality, style, likes and professional interests to your network. In this way, you will be more likely to capture the help you need, when you need it.

As one famous author on the subject, Keith Ferrazzi (2005) once said "The best time to build a network is before you need it."

New managers, when talking about building a network, often make the mistake of first looking upwards – surely it is those "up there" who can be of most help. Do not only look upwards – go for everyone. Everyone is a potential network member. Often it is the people that you least expect to be of help that provide you with the introduction or direction that you need.

Rule 2: Give, give, give!

It feels really good when you are able to help someone else. But there is another reason for giving. When you give, people are more likely to give back. In fact the social psychologists have a term for it, "reciprocity". The research clearly shows that the more you give of yourself, the more likely people are to help you when you need it.

You might be saying, "Yes, that's OK, but how do I give? How will people come to me? Why should they?" Become an expert – "Build the field and they will come".

Rule 3: Make contact with your potential network members

Members of your network should be both within your organisation and external to it. Internal network members are more likely to be of help with getting things done, whilst external members are more likely to be of help in developing your knowledge and expertise. Additionally, both will be of considerable help in developing and progressing your career.

How do you make contact with potential members? Here are some suggestions – you'll probably think of some more as you read through the list.

- When next you are in an interdepartmental meeting or project team meeting, make contact with someone who has impressed you and suggest that you get together for a coffee.
- Ask your boss for the names of some of the people outside of your department that could be of help to you. Call them up and arrange to meet. Make sure you have a topic to discuss, or if you are new to the organisation, you could ask for their advice on navigating your way through the organisational deep waters.
- Arrange to meet with key customers or suppliers of your department or organisation. Always make sure you know as much as possible about your contact before meeting them.
- Regularly attend professional / industry events. Make a point of making contact with at least two people at each event. These are people that you will call later and meet with and are in addition to all the people with whom you will swap business cards during the event.
- Join Industry and professional or trade associations, local chambers of commerce. Make contact with at least two people with whom you will later meet.
- Join special interest group committees, or if your time does not per-

mit, offer to speak at their sessions or conferences. Once again, make contact with at least two people with whom you will later meet.

- Finally, develop yourself as an expert in a particular field. Become known both inside and outside the organisation as someone "who knows a lot about that". In this way, people will start to beat a path to your door.

Keep in mind that building your network happens one person at a time. For instance, when my wife recently started with her new employer where there were some 70,000 employees worldwide, she realised that it would be her ability to build her network rather than her managerial or technical expertise that would set her up for success. She worked out a plan of meeting with one new person from outside her department every week. People tell other people. After a year in the role, she is now known as an expert in her area of expertise around the world!

Rule 4: Keep in touch to maintain your network

Making the first contact is obviously important. However, keeping in contact over the longer term is the only way to maintain your network. This requires some discipline. If you are that way inclined, then you're off to a flying start. If not, then make your diary work for you – e.g. all of the computer planning and diary systems have the ability to enter people's names and follow up dates, so use these aids.

Some ideas for keeping in touch …

- Draw up a list of your contacts.
- Make a note to stay in touch on a regular basis. A minimum time is every three months.
- Diary to contact a certain number of your network members every week. In this way, you can spread the load evenly throughout each quarter.
- Send people emails on areas of interest to them.
- When you come across an article or website that may be of interest to someone, send them the details.
- Invite people to coffee or lunch.
- Put people in touch with other people who may have similar interests or needs.

Keith Ferrazzi author of "Never Eat Alone: And Other Secrets to Success, One Relationship at a Time" (Currency, 2005) says, "Great networkers have the implicit understanding that investing time and energy in building personal relationships with the right people will pay dividends. In fact, the top people all understand this dynamic. They themselves used the power of their network of contacts and friends to arrive at their present station."

Influencing – a real benefit!

As a colleague once said to me "I've noticed a real side benefit to influencing. People like being around people who use their influencing skills well. Good influencers seem to exude a sense that things happen when they're about. They don't sit around wishing things were different whilst moaning there's nothing they can do about it. Nor do they blame others or complain about what needs fixing. They see what needs doing and set about getting it done."

HOW TO IMPLEMENT THE IDEAS IN THIS CHAPTER

☞ How to start influencing, straight away

I suggest the best way to start influencing more effectively is to use more of the opening up behaviours, Reflecting and Questioning. As you develop skill with these, you can move onto Asserting and Suggesting.

The reason for starting with the openers is that they force you to get into the other person's world. Once there, this will give you a far better opportunity to influence as you will know and focus on, their needs and interests.

1. When you talk with someone who has an issue or problem that is upsetting them (i.e. it is affecting their feelings) practise using **Reflecting** . . .

Really *listen* to the underlying message being expressed by the *other person*:

*   Be genuine. Listen. Hold judgment. Do not give your opinion.

- Make listening noises, e.g., "uh huh", "ok", "I see", etc. or nod to indicate you are really interested and want the other person to continue.

- <u>Repeat</u> what the other person has <u>said.</u>

- <u>Rephrase</u> what the other person has <u>said.</u>

- <u>Summarise</u> what the other person is <u>feeling.</u>

- Ask the other person how they *feel* about the topic.

- Reflect the <u>other person's feelings</u> back to them in your own words.

2. When you find yourself in a discussion over a difference of opinion, practise using Questioning by asking fact-finding, ***non-judgmental questions*** to gather data and information from the ***other person***:

- Ask questions using "How? What? When? Where? & Why?"

- Develop the use of both open and closed questions.

- Ask fact finding questions.

- Ask for the reasons or theories behind the other person's statements or proposals.

 How to become an expert influencer

- Start working on using more of the openers, Reflecting and Questioning, in your discussions with people (as outlined above).

- Build and plan to maintain your network.

How to Start your Network . . .

1. Take a sheet of paper and split it into 3 columns.

1. Contacts that I know:	2. Who introduced me to this person?	3. To whom did I introduce this person?

2. Look for the person whose name keeps recurring in column 2 – these are good networkers. You need to develop more of these to increase your own network because they will work for you.

3. If "Self" appears frequently in column 2, you do not yet have enough "networkers" that can help you build your network.

4. If you do not have many names in column 3, then you yourself are not yet networking hard enough. Remember, one of the rules was "Give, give, give!" You will now need to start more networking:

- Make contact with someone who has impressed you and suggest that you get together for a coffee or lunch.

- Ask your boss for the names of some of the people outside of your department that could be of help to you. Call them up and arrange to meet.

- Arrange to meet with key customers or suppliers of your department.

- Attend professional / industry events. Make a point of making contact with at least two people at each event. Contact these people after the event.

- Join special interest group committees, or if your time does not permit, offer to speak at their sessions or conferences.

- Add one person to your network every week. (Using this approach over the last six months, I have built my own network to 253 people! People know people, who know people. And so it goes and grows)

5. Categorise your network

As you start to develop your network, it is important to have a balance between external and internal. It is also a good idea to categorise your contacts into:

- Task / Technical / Professional – these are the people that can help you build your professional expertise and reputation.
- Career – these are the people that may be useful in helping you develop your career to its full potential.
- Social – these are the people that will help you maintain a balance in your life.
- You can draw up a matrix similar to the following …

	Task / Tech / Prof.	Career	Social
Internal			
External			

- Make sure you have a balance between External / Internal and Task / Career / Social.

6. Set up a diary system to ensure that you maintain contact with your network members at least quarterly. Diary to contact a certain number of your network members every week.

Chapter 12

How to Manage Your Boss

W hen we think about "managing" it's normal to think about managing people who report directly to you. But there is another very important person you must manage if you yourself are to become an effective manager – your boss. Chapters One and Two outlined some techniques and strategies for improving your managerial role elements of leading, managing and operating. If you've started on these and involved your boss as was suggested, then you're off to a good start by making some very positive impressions on your boss.

In addition to what you may have already done or be doing with your boss by way of creating a good impression, there are some very positive things that you can consciously do to manage your boss and the relationship you have with him or her. These are summarised as "rules to live by" that you should always follow and "steps to take" that you can start implementing immediately.

Four rules to live by - and - Four steps to take to effectively manage your boss

The case of Bob's boss, John

John was a former boss of mine. Before I started working for him, I had heard from others that he had a good reputation and so I was really looking forward to working with him. The office was a very busy one with lots of customer interaction and a heavy processing workload. After the first couple of months, I got the feeling that there was no real harmony in our relationship and I found it difficult to work out why. John was good with the customers and well liked by other staff, but John and I just didn't seem to hit it off.

It was not until my formal performance appraisal some months later that

166

I finally found out what the problem was. The job I'd taken over was in a real mess and required a great deal of people and administrative management skill to get it back on track, which I believed I had done well. During my performance appraisal discussion, John acknowledged my good work in this area, but (and it was a big "but" for him) he didn't see me doing enough marketing with potential customers.

You see, John's pet interest was marketing and he expected all of his people to make marketing their number one priority. I on the other hand, considered that getting the management of the people and the processes right was the more critical need.

Do you know what your manager's number one or key priorities are?

Although we often have performance discussions with our manager;

- How clear are you on the order of priority your manager has for each area of your performance?
- How clear do you think your manager is about his/her expectations of you?

These expectations are often unwritten and in fact may be somewhat different to the formal performance requirements of your role.

So, what's the best way to manage the relationship with your boss?

There are two components to this; firstly four clear action steps that you can plan for and take at the start of your working partnership. These include identifying his or her priorities. Secondly, four "rules" that you should follow in all your dealings with your boss to ensure an ongoing, productive working relationship is maintained.

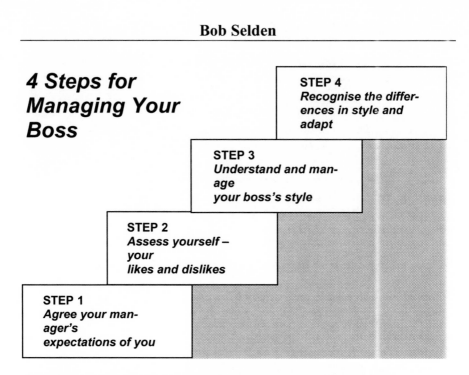

4 Steps for Managing Your Boss

STEP 4
Recognise the differences in style and adapt

STEP 3
Understand and manage your boss's style

STEP 2
Assess yourself – your likes and dislikes

STEP 1
Agree your manager's expectations of you

Step One: Agree your manager's expectations of you

A simple way of doing this, is to have a discussion with him or her, preferably soon after you start in the role. Ask your manager;

- "What are the top three priorities in the role that you would like me to focus on?"

Or, if you have a formal performance discussion;

- Ask your manager to assign a percentage figure of "importance" against each one of your key responsibility areas so that you can assess his or her priorities. Each key responsibility should be given a percentage out of a total for all areas of 100%, or if you like, points out of 100. You should also ask when discussing each responsibility "Why is this so important?" The answer will give you a host of good clues for developing the relationship with your manager. These clues are most likely your boss' unwritten expectations.

Here's an actual example that one manager in the Risk Management team in a financial services organisation set for a senior team member:

Objective	Weighting	Target
1. Risk management	30 points	Handling risk aspects for the ABC & XYZ fund range under your main area of responsibility to the agreed standards and objectives as set out by the Head of RM.
2. Project completion	25 points	Completing the Zero Sum and Akka projects within the deadlines and to the standards agreed and set.
3. Team collaboration	20 points	<ul><li>Taking an active role in the team by readily sharing your experience with the other team members on a daily basis and during meetings, and being prepared to accept feedback from them.</li><li>Being the back-up for the Head of Risk Management for one detailed internal contact/meeting per month.</li></ul>
4. Knowledge development	15 points	<ul><li>Completing the assessment test for the R.M. handbook with 100% accuracy.</li><li>Attending a minimum of two R.M. conferences and presenting a list of critical learning issues to the team.</li></ul>
5. Participate in maintaining team performance	10 points	Identifying problems/issues that may affect team performance and proposing solutions in a timely manner so that team performance is not jeopardized.

Here's another approach taken by an HR Director reporting to the CEO .
. .

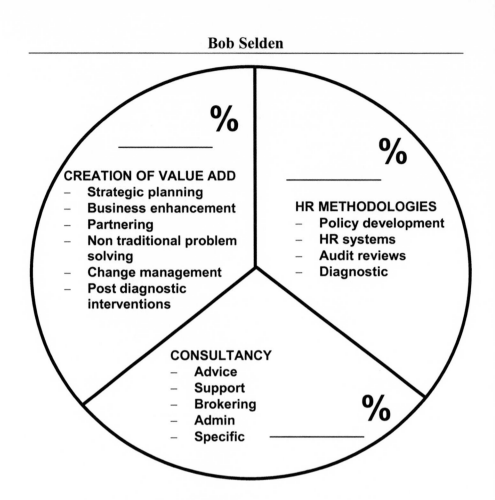

If your discussion with your manager is still merely a repeat of the formal performance requirements of your role, or you sense there is more information lurking behind the answer to your question "Why is this area so important?", you may need to dig a little deeper.

Remember, sometimes your boss may not even be consciously aware of these unwritten expectations, but none the less they will be there. One good way of digging these out, is to ask him or her to describe their ideal employee. You can do this with questions such as:

- "You've probably had many good people working for you previously. What is it about these people that you particularly liked?" or,

- "Tell me about the best person you've ever had working for you"

If you want some more information, you can always ask your manager to describe some of the characteristics and behaviours of their most disappointing employees. For example:

- "Tell me about the worst person you've ever had working for you"

Step Two: Assess yourself – your likes and dislikes

What is it about you that impedes or facilitates you working with your boss?

Draw up a (short) list of:

- "Things that I like about working with my boss" and
- "Things that I don't like about working with my boss".

Work out some ways to overcome, or at least manage, the things that you don't like. Although these are things that you don't like, they are probably the areas that your boss is also least happy with. If necessary, ask some of your peers for assistance, particularly those who seem to have a good relationship with him or her.

You should also review the information about your manager's ideal employee and most disappointing employee that you obtained in step one. What will you need to do to ensure that you take account of your manager's likes and dislikes in his or her employees?

Applying this step doesn't mean that you have to change your style or personality. However, it does mean that you need to be careful that your behaviour does not clash with your manager's expectations.

Step Three: Understand and manage your boss's style

You don't have to become lifelong friends with your boss, but you do have to understand him or her. For example, try to develop strategies for the following:

- *How does he/she like to receive information? When? What form? Does he/she like lots of detail or big picture? Give it that way.*

- *What is his/her number one strength? Capitalise on it.*

- *What is his/her number one weakness? How can you help?*

- *What's the boss' central goal? How can you assist?*

- *What are his/her main pressures? How can you help minimize these?*

- *How does your boss handle conflict? How can you help? Can you work out a productive way to cope with situations where you and your boss may disagree?*

Step Four: Recognise that there are differences in style and adapt

You and your boss may have different personality styles; you may be an introvert, your boss may be an extrovert, or vice versa. This doesn't mean that you suddenly have to change, but please do think about his or her style and learn to manage the style. For instance, extroverts like to work out problems by talking them through. So, if your boss is more extroverted, then it can be quite useful to talk through issues with him or her to reach a decision. Introverts on the other hand, like plenty of time to think about a problem and then discuss their ideas and possible solutions. If your boss is more introverted, then you will need to go to him or her with very well thought out proposals and recommendations – trying to reach a conclusion by talking a range of issues through with this style of manager will definitely not work.

Make sure that you have a good understanding of both yours and your boss' style so that you can learn to manage the differences.

Implementing these four steps with your boss will go a long way to building a solid foundation for the relationship. In addition, there are also four rules that you should always follow in your ongoing relationship with your boss if you want the relationship to be truly productive.

Rule One: There should be no surprises, ever!

Keep your boss informed of what's happening in your area on a regular basis, particularly potential problems. If you are in doubt as to what to tell or not tell, always ask yourself: "Would this information have an impact on my boss' position?" It's generally better to communicate too much than too little.

Rule Two: Never hide a problem

No matter how much you try, hidden problems will always come back to bite you They are like lies – they will always find you out. Far better to be proactive. Keep in mind that you will help your situation if you present the information in a style that suits your boss. Try to get the words right by communicating in a style that suits your boss' communication style.

Rule Three: Always do your homework

Before approaching your boss with a question or to ask for help, always do as much research as possible so that you have the complete facts. If he or she constantly has to send you away for more information, then you have not prepared properly. Try to bring your solutions or suggested solutions with you when presenting a problem on which you want some help. This will demonstrate to your boss that you are taking initiative although you may not have all the answers just yet. Your problem should be well-thought-out, even though your solution may not be.

Rule Four: Do not underrate or undercut your boss

Present a united front – support your boss with others. Disagree with him/her in private, never in public.

Finally, remember the person who has most control over your immediate future other than yourself, is your boss. Treat him or her with that respect. From my experience, following these four rules and implementing the four steps mentioned earlier, will ensure that your relationship with your boss is a very positive one.

For instance, by following these boss management strategies with my manager John, I was able to turn around what had started out as a poor relationship. So much so, that when I decided to resign some time later to take up a better job offer, John tried hard to keep me as I had become one of his "ideal employees".

In summary . . .

To become a successful manager, you must not only be effective in terms of achieving what is expected of you, you must also be "seen" to be effective, particularly by your boss. To be seen as effective by your boss means actively managing the relationship between you and your boss.

HOW TO IMPLEMENT THE IDEAS IN THIS CHAPTER

🏳 **How to start Managing Your Boss straight away**

1. Set aside some time to think through the following four steps.
2. Take a sheet of paper and list the answers to the associated questions.

Steps to take . . .	Write out your answers to these questions:
1. Agree your manager's expectations of you	• What are his/her top 3 or 4 priorities for you? Weight these. • What are his/her unwritten expectations of you? • If you cannot answer the above questions, have a discussion with your boss to find out what are his/her priorities.
2. Assess your own likes and dislikes	• What is it that you like/don't like about working for your boss? • How can you best manage these?
3. Understand and manage your boss' style	• How does he/she like to communicate? • Strengths/weaknesses? • His/her goals/objectives? • The way he/she manages pressure/conflict?
4. Recognise that there are differences in style and adapt	• Is he/she introverted/extraverted? • Base your communication on his/her style.

3. Make a note in your diary once a month for the next six months to review your answers to ensure you are implementing your boss management strategy. At the same time, do a quick check to ensure you are following these four rules.

What To Do When You Become The Boss

Rules to live by . . .	How to live the rules . . .
1. There should be no surprises for your boss – ever!	• Keep your manager informed of what is happening in your area and particularly things that are likely to impact him/her or other areas.
2. Never hide a problem	• Advise him/her of potential problems in plenty of time. • Communicate in a style that suits him/her.
3. Always do your homework	• When approaching your boss with an issue, gather all the facts. • Try to present possible solutions when you take a problem to him/her.
4. Do not underrate or undercut your boss	• Support your boss with others. • Disagree with him/her in private, face to face, never in public.

Chapter 13

How To Select Your New Boss

A four pronged boss selection strategy

Have you had an experience where you found out after starting in a new role that your boss was not all that you thought he or she might be? Or maybe you are in the process of applying for a new job right now? (Probably not a good idea to show this chapter to your current boss!)

Jane's new boss

Jane had been out of the country for over a year and returned home to start a new job as a physiotherapist in a family run business. She was excited about the new role as the husband and wife team who ran the practice had been asking her for some time to join them as a full time employee.

During the first week, Jane did not have as many patients as the other physiotherapists, so she was asked to work less hours. This seemed fair as it does take time to build a personal clientele. However in her second week, it became obvious that Jane's expected full time job was to be part time. Her bosses were setting her up to work part time hours. She also started to get a bit uneasy about her new boss' management styles. Firstly they seemed unwilling to talk about her hours. Then, she found her patient files had been examined without asking her, nor had she been given any subsequent feedback, either positive or negative. Jane is someone who likes to be involved and communicated with. Her ideal job had started to lose its shine.

When applying for a new job, you are rightly concerned about putting your best foot forward and making sure that you are selected. However, sometimes we neglect the fact that selection is a two way street – they select you as an employee and you select them as an employer.

How desperate are you for a job? Even if you are desperate now, is a job with a bad boss better than waiting and working through more interviews until you find the right boss? After all, if you accept an offer of a job with a bad boss, statistics tell us you will soon resign.

At the time of writing, the employment market currently favours the employee, so you have a great many options open to you. Take your time. At the end of this chapter, there is a comprehensive checklist to assist in your selection process.

Unfortunately, the consequences of not selecting the right boss only become obvious once you are in the new role. My research clearly shows that people rarely leave an organisation, they leave a boss. It is therefore vital that when you apply for a position, you not only look at the organisation and the role, but you also interview your boss with as much thoroughness as he or she interviews you.

How do you interview your prospective boss, particularly when the focus of the employment interview is the other way round?

1.   Decide on your selection criteria

Well, before you even get to the interview, it's very useful to jot down what your selection criteria are for an effective boss. You should do this in much the same way as you would if you were a manager selecting a new employee.

When you have drawn up your selection criteria, place them in priority order. This is so that you can make a sound and realistic assessment of your potential boss' ability to manage you in the style which best suits you.

Once you are clear on your criteria, weave them into the selection interview.

2.   Look for clues during the interview

You may get some idea of how your future boss operates by the way the interview is conducted. For example, how comfortable did you feel during the interview? What impression did he / she make on you?

3. Find out what your prospective boss' ideal employee looks like

When the interview gets to the "Do you have any questions?" stage, here are some questions you might like to ask. The aim here is to get him/her to describe their ideal employee to you.

For example, you might ask; "You've probably had some very good employees working for you. What is it about them that made them so good?" Of course, you can also ask about his or her poor employees as well. Put the two together and you now have a very good description of what your prospective boss might call "ideal".

The answers the boss gives will be about the things he or she looks for and how they judge their employees. Most importantly, their answers will show how he or she manages their employees. Look for signs during their answers that tell you about your selection criteria, such as autonomy, responsibility, initiative, communication and so on.

4. Assess your prospective boss against your selection criteria

You should have a question ready for at least each of your three most important selection criteria. For example, if "autonomy" is a key need for you, your question may be something like "Autonomy is important to me as I find it very motivating. Can you please give me an example of how you manage the level of autonomy you give your people?" Or perhaps if "training" is important for you, your question might be "I like to learn as much as I can about the job and the organisation. Can you please give me an example of the training or coaching you provide for your people?"

In all of your boss selection questions, keep asking for examples to illustrate. Examples describe what the boss does and says with his/her employees. With enough examples, you can develop a very good idea of your prospective boss' management style.

Finally, if your interview throws up some doubts in your mind about the prospect of a positive relationship with your prospective boss, my advice would be to "pass" on this role and look for another opportunity. Try not to become too seduced by the excitement of the role, the salary or the conditions. Ultimately, all of these will pale by comparison with the on-going relationship you have with your boss.

Keep in mind that it's a selection interview – for both of you.

HOW TO IMPLEMENT THE IDEAS IN THIS CHAPTER

⚑ **How to select your new boss**

Steps to take . . .	Ideas to consider . . .
1. Decide on your Boss Selection Criteria	• Think back to previous good bosses that you have had. What made them good for you?
	• Conversely, think of the reasons why some previous bosses have not been so good. Avoid these at all costs.
	• How much autonomy do you like in your job?
	• How much feedback do you like to get about your performance? How do you like this feedback given?
	• How much responsibility do you like to be given?
	• Are you a very practical person, or more creative? How should your boss manage this?
	• How do you like to be trained and coached?
	• How do you like your boss to communicate with you?
	• Finally, place your criteria in priority order.
2. Look for clues during the interview	• Did it start and finish on time? Is this important to you?
	• How courteous was your prospective boss? Did this have an impact on you?
	• Did he/she allow you the opportunity to put your point without talking over the top of you? How well listened to did you feel?
	• Did he/she discuss examples of previous employees in a confidential manner?
	• Did he/she explain the performance require-

	ments of the role? Did you gain a very clear idea of what will be expected of you in the role?
	• Was the room layout formal or informal? Did this matter to you?
	• Finally, from the examples and explanations given, what management style do you believe your prospective boss has? Does this match your ideal?
3. Find out what your prospective boss' ideal employee looks like	• Ask "Can you tell me about some of the better employees you have had? What made them so good?", or
	• "What do you look for in an employee?"
4. Assess your prospective boss against your selection criteria	• Make sure you have three questions that relate directly to your selection criteria.
	• Also make sure to ask for examples that relate to your selection criteria.
	• After the interview, assess your prospective boss' responses against your selection criteria.

Part 4: Managing Your Meetings

One-on-one is ok, but how do you influence people in groups?

In Part 3, we discussed how to influence others. Often this was on a one-on-one basis. You'll not be surprised to see that many of those same skills can be applied as well to group situations. However, whenever you meet with more than one person, the complexity of the communication and how to manage the communication process, increases dramatically. You may need to adjust your communication skills for this different context.

Many new managers (and unfortunately quite a number of more experienced managers as well), are quite good when it comes to communicating with one person, but are less successful when faced with group situations.

Why aren't these managers able to transfer their one-on-one skills to the group? There are two possible reasons:

1. A lack of understanding of group processes and how groups work, and
2. A lack of focus (or sometimes inability) to manage the group process.

Part 4 is about process. What is "process" and how to manage it. The more effective managers are really good at process management. In fact, these are generally the managers that also progress well through the organisation. It is their ability to process manage that enables them to manage areas or units where often the people they are managing are far more technically or professionally knowledgeable and experienced than the manager.

Learning tips to help you get the most out of Part 4 . . .

There are two chapters in Part 4:

- *Chapter 14: Group and Team Decision Making* "What are the various ways groups and leaders make decisions?"
- *Chapter 15: How to get the best out of your Meetings* "How to plan, run and evaluate the effectiveness of your meetings"

Theorists and **Reflectors** will want to read each in its entirety.

Process management is such an important skill to develop that it is suggested that **Activists** and **Pragmatists** read Chapter 14 in its entirety and complete the activity. You should then use Chapter 15 to re-think how you run your meetings – in particular, go to the activity at the end of the chapter on "Team Process Evaluation".

Enjoy!

Chapter 14
Group and Team Decision Making

Do you need to gain commitment or compliance from your group or team?

Rob and Compliance

Rob worked as a qualified, but junior physiotherapist in a busy hospital. He along with three of his colleagues were asked by their manager to discuss amongst themselves how they would like their rosters to be organised (i.e. who would do what shifts etc.) and put forward their proposal. Rob and his colleagues were very happy with their final choices. They had considered all of their personal and professional needs and felt that their decision was the best for all.

A day before the new rosters were to start, Rob found out by rumour during his lunch break that their roster recommendations were not to be implemented. Worse still, the rosters decided on by their manager did not suit any of the four. This decision by their manager resulted in a severe lowering of morale within the team and created a culture of mistrust toward their manager. In future, they would be very wary of any suggestion or request for their input from management.

Have you ever been a member of a work team where the manager threw a difficult problem over to the team to solve, only to see the manager implement a completely different decision to the one the team came up with? If the implemented solution affected the ongoing congruence and cohesiveness of the team, how did this make you feel? Why does this happen? Is it a legitimate management strategy for group decision making?

Often this occurs because:

- the manager does not understand the importance and nature of group decision making within teams, or
- the manager has a level of comfort with one particular style of team decision making irrespective of the circumstances or context of the problem.

Decision making within groups ranges along a continuum;

- at one end, "by the leader with little or no discussion",
- through to "complete consensus" at the other.

Some very useful work on group decision making was carried out by Vroom and Yetton (1973). The following continuum of group decision making is based on their studies.

A continuum of group decision making

Here are the seven stages along the Decision Making Continuum:

Autocratic	Consultative	Expert	Averaging	Minority	Majority	Consensus
By the leader with little or no discussion	By the leader following group consultation	By an "expert" either within the group or advice received by the group	Averaging e.g. using a mathematic process to assess options, then averaging	By a minority - can be through personal or positional power	By majority vote - can be either formal or informal	Full consensus

Each method of decision making has its place and can be a very successful method. As a manager, the method of group decision making you decide on, depends on a number of factors such as:

- What are the time pressures on both you and the team?
- How important or otherwise is the final decision to the team?
- Does the team have the skill or expertise to make the decision?
- Who in the team needs to be involved? How much team involvement is necessary?

- Finally, and probably one of the most important considerations, is; "Do you want commitment or do you only need compliance from the team?"

Of the seven group decision making methods, "consensus" is the most likely to produce commitment to the team decision. Using the other six methods should bring compliance because of your position as their manager. Team commitment will then depend on:

- How well you are perceived as a leader by team members
- How effective (for all concerned) is the final decision

← *Compliance through power*				*More likely to gain commitment* →		
Autocratic	Consultative	Expert	Averaging	Minority	Majority	Consensus

Consensus is often put forward by many managerial experts as the most appropriate for team decision making. The argument, and it is a good one, is that consensus decision making is far more likely to build a feeling of good staff morale.

Consensus has also been found to be a more rigorous process and often more accurate than some of the other methods. This is supported by the study of jury decision making, where groups are required to make some very important decisions. For instance, juries required to make unanimous decisions consider the evidence more carefully and thoroughly and report higher levels of juror confidence in the ultimate decision, than juries operating a majority verdict system.

In terms of accuracy, a recent study of the difference between judges' opinions of the probable outcome of 48 trials (ranging from a day to five weeks duration) and the ultimate outcome decided by the actual juries using the consensus method, resulted in only three differences (Law Reform Commission of NSW 2001).

So when, rigor, accuracy and commitment to the final decision are important, the consensus method brings the best results.

However, if you do not need commitment, but merely compliance, then it can be legitimate and effective to choose a method other than consensus.

Sometimes this may be necessary because of time, context or other pressures. For example, it would be inappropriate (and quite hazardous) for an army officer to hold a group consensus meeting with the troops on how to hold back the imminent approach of the enemy.

Which is the best for you?

To gain a better understanding of the merits of each method, their plusses and minuses are listed in the following table.

1. Decisions made by the leader without group consultation

AUTOCRATIC *By the Leader - no discussion*	• Efficient in terms of time used. • The group has to act on the decision, as involvement is minimal. Commitment therefore will depend on faith in, or relationship to, the leader. • Not all members may understand the decision and therefore not be able to implement the decision.

2. Decisions made by the leader following group consultation

CONSULTATIVE
 	
By the leader - after discussion
	• The accuracy of the leader's decision is usually improved.
	• The greater the leader's listening skills, the better will be the decision.
	• Members participate in the discussion, but not in the decision.
	• Members can at times tend to either:
	   – compete to impress the leader, or
	   – tell the leader what they think he/she wants to hear.

3. Decisions made by an expert in the subject matter

EXPERT *By an "expert"*	• Who is the expert? They must be credible. • Personal power and popularity often cloud the selection of the expert. • Unless there is very clearly an expert on the subject who is seen as such by the group, this method often fails. • This method does not involve the group in the decision.

4. Decisions made by averaging decisions of individuals

AVERAGING *By using some form of mathematical averaging*	• The group decision may be determined by less than 30% of the members. Research shows that the most common decision is not necessarily held by more than half of the members. • At least the members are consulted, but they do not take part in the final decision. • The opinions of the least knowledgeable may annul the opinions of the most knowledgeable. • Commitment to the final decision is not very strong, and hence effectiveness of decision may be slight.

5. Decisions made by a minority of the members

MINORITY *Minority*	• The majority may not be committed to the decision. • The majority may try not to implement the decision. • Can be time efficient. • Decisions are not often the best decisions.

6. Decisions made by taking the majority vote

MAJORITY *Majority vote*	• Often splits a group into 'winners' and 'losers'. • 'Losers' may try to subvert the decision, particularly where emotions are involved. • Encourages either/or when there may be better alternatives. • Fosters blind arguments rather than rational decisions. • Can be dangerous when total group commitment to the decision is required. • When commitment by everyone is not essential, this method can work well.

7. Decisions made by group consensus

CONSENSUS *Through discussion, the group works to reach consensus*	• Most thorough means of examining all the options, but also takes the most time. • All members understand the decision and are prepared to support the decision. • Allows people to disagree, but through discussion reach a stage at which they can say "I can live with that" (understanding). • All members have full time to both agree and disagree with others' views. • Higher quality decisions result. • Differences of opinion force the group to seek better alternatives. • Decisions are not always easy to achieve, but group commitment is high.

	• Higher levels of conflict often occur. As a result, more alternatives are tabled in efforts to resolve this conflict.
	• Can prove frustrating to the leader.
	• Often the more time taken in reaching the decision by consensus, reduces the time needed to implement.

The Golden Rule of Team Decision Making?
"Always inform your team beforehand how the decision will be made"

For example, if you decide that in a particular case, this is your decision to make but you would like the input of your team in order to make an informed decision (Method 2: By the leader following group consultation), say so. You will find that if you tell the team on all occasions, then the team will become more involved and ultimately committed to, or at least accepting of, both the decision making process and the decisions themselves.

* **Your own style?**

All of the above sounds reasonable and logical and it is. Now, here's the kicker. It's most likely that you will already have developed a preferred style (method) that you use on most occasions. For example, through experience and feedback, I've found out that my own natural style is "consensus". That's mostly OK in my role as an organisational consultant where I need to get group commitment to the final decision. However, it has its drawbacks. People have sometimes seen this as weak and too time consuming. Undoubtedly, there have been times in the past where it would have been more appropriate given the circumstances, for me to adopt another method.

Have a look back over the seven methods. What do you think your natural style is? Is it always appropriate in your circumstances to use this method? Do you over-use one or two methods and under-use others?

You should consider what your preferred style of group decision making is and most importantly, how appropriate is it for the current situation. A quick way of assessing your natural style is to think for a moment about the last 5 or 6 meetings you have run with your team where there was a critical decision to make:

- What style of decision making as a leader did you adopt?
- What style do you feel most comfortable with?

It is suggested that you read the list again prior to each team meeting and decide at the outset what method you will adopt for this meeting and this decision. This will prevent you from becoming locked into your natural or preferred method. Remember to let your team know how the final decision will be made and why it will be made that way.

Above all, having decided on a method for this particular decision, stick with it. In the case of Rob's manager mentioned at the start of this chapter, you can see that she adopted consensus as the most appropriate and effective method initially, but then changed her mind after the event. Initial commitment was certainly lost, grudging compliance was gained and it's a good bet that staff morale in her team would be very low for some considerable time to come.

HOW TO IMPLEMENT THE IDEAS IN THIS CHAPTER

☞ **How to start making the most effective Team Decisions straight away**

Decision parameters to consider ...	Decision methods and possible consequences to consider ...
Are you under extreme time constraints?	• Consider a method other than consensus. • Remember, you may gain compliance but not necessarily commitment.
How important or otherwise is the final decision to the team?	• If it is important, consider consensus as your possible first choice. • Remember, it will take time.
Does the team have the skill or expertise to make the decision?	• If not, consider using the services of an expert. • Remember, you will need to sell the decision and the expert to your team.
Who in the team needs to be involved?	• You may be able to hand it over to a sub group (minority). • Remember, you will need to sell the decision and the decision making process, to your team.
How much team involvement is needed?	• If not everyone needs (or wants) to be involved, you may consider any of the six methods other than consensus. • If the decision will affect other team members, you will need to inform them and ultimately, sell the final decision.
Do you want commitment from the team?	• Consensus would be the best way to go. • Remember, it will take time.

Remember:

"Always inform your team beforehand how the decision will be made"

☞ **How to keep making the most effective team decisions**

1. **Find out what your natural style is**. You may do this by:
   - Asking some of your colleagues who have seen you run meetings.
   - Alternatively, ask them to sit in on some of your meetings.
   - If you've built up a good reputation and rapport with your team, you could show then the seven decision making styles and ask which one they see you using most often.

2. **Prior to each critical decision that may affect the team:**
   - Read through the seven methods and decide which is most appropriate in this situation.
   - Advise the team how the final decision will be made.

Chapter 15

How to get the best out of your Meetings

Why are so many meetings such a waste of time?

How often have you sat in a meeting thinking "This is such a waste of time. I have so many others things to do. I wish I could be somewhere else." Sound familiar? We've all probably had these thoughts at one time or another and maybe for some of us, it has been very recent.

One of the most common complaints heard from all levels, is "We waste so much time here sitting around talking. Nothing gets done as a result". Why do people feel that so many meetings are a waste of time?

Ineffective meetings:

- Cover information that could be distributed by other means
- Focus too much on the past – what has gone rather than what is to come
- Do not have a clearly defined purpose with intended outcomes

As a new manager, you'll need to run meetings to:

- Keep people informed
- Find out how well the team is operating
- Ensure that all views have been considered before making decisions
- Maximize commitment to decisions being made
- Solve problems that will affect the group
- Help keep people motivated and focused

- Train and develop people to reach their full potential

Meetings – information or problem solving?

The first decision to make is to decide what type of meeting it is –

- Is this an **information sharing** meeting? or
- A **problem solving** meeting?

1.   Information sharing meetings

Information sharing meetings are conducted to ensure that everybody who needs to know something has had the opportunity to hear and understand what he or she needs to know.

For **information sharing meetings**, there are three points to consider:

1.   What is the purpose of the meeting and who should be involved?
2.   Can the information be distributed in another way (e.g. email etc)? In this case there is no need for the meeting, thus saving a lot of time.
3.   If the need to share the information must be by way of a meeting, then the focus of the meeting (and time spent) should be
   - 20% past oriented - i.e. reporting on the information (e.g. results) and
   - 80% future oriented – i.e. deciding what we are going to do with the information.

Using the "80/20 rule" for your information sharing meetings will ensure that everyone participates and can see some real advantage to having the meeting.

Keep in mind, that this is an information sharing meeting. However, if decisions do need to be made on certain issues, let the group know how these decisions will be made. That is, as their manager, will the decision be made:

By you with little or no discussion from the group?	By you following consultation with the group?	By an "expert" either within the group or advice received by the group?	By averaging e.g. using a mathematic process to assess options, then averaging?	By a minority - can be through personal or positional power?	By majority vote - can be either formal or informal?	By full consensus?
Autocratic	*Consultative*	*Expert*	*Averaging*	*Minority*	*Majority*	*Consensus*

By the way, if you are a participant in one of those boring meetings mentioned earlier, it is possible to have some influence on the meeting process. Keep asking:

- "OK, so what are we going to do with this information?" or,
- "We've heard the background, so how should we proceed now?".

In other words, every time the meeting starts to focus on the past, redirect it to the future.

2. Problem solving meetings

Problem solving meetings are conducted to gather everyone's views on a problem; get their involvement on solving the problem; and to gain their commitment to implement the most workable solutions. So, running a problem solving meeting will be more challenging than an information sharing meeting. For example, they will certainly require more thought and planning.

One of the nice by-products for you in running problem solving meetings, is the development of your own leadership skills. It's probably fair to say that the better you become at running problem solving meetings, the more you will be recognised as a leader by your people. Your people will judge you very critically by the way you run a problem solving meeting. For instance, they will be (privately) asking:

- How well did my manager involve people in the problem analysis and solution?
- Did my manager listen to everybody, or just put his/her opinion?
- Did I feel that all views were accepted for discussion?

- Was my manager able to identify the key issues and explain them so that everyone understood?
- Was any conflict that arose managed effectively?
- Did my manager regularly summarise our progress so that we knew what had been covered?
- How efficiently was time used?
- Did I feel committed to the final decision?

For **problem solving meetings**, there are three factors to consider to ensure the meeting is a positive one with some productive outcomes:

1. What is the purpose of the meeting and who should be involved? i.e. What is the problem to be solved? Who will need to have input to the problem analysis and/or solution? Who will need to be committed to implementing the solution?

2. What decision making style will you adopt? Remember, as this is a problem solving meeting, commitment is most likely to be gained when a consensus decision making process is used. Do you need full commitment to the problem solution?

3. How will you facilitate the meeting? For example, will you lead the meeting? Will you share leadership? Will you have another member lead the meeting?

As with Information sharing meetings, often problem solving meetings don't reach their full potential because the meeting dwells too much on the present or past situation, rather than "how things ought to be."

However, problem solving meetings are quite different in both style and context. With information sharing meetings, as the manager you set yourself up as the group's boss – you have the formal authority over the group – you have some information they need to hear and understand. Although there will often be plenty of discussion around various items, because it's an information sharing meeting, you are seen by the members to have formal control over both the topics and the group. They will most likely defer to your decision.

With problem solving meetings on the other hand, your role becomes very much more of a facilitator – you are facilitating some action to take place. The success of your problem solving meeting will therefore depend more on how you manage the meeting rather than the fact that you are their formal manager.

Before discussing how to run these types of meetings, it's worthwhile looking at the word "facilitate" – your understanding will impact your decisions about how to run the meeting.

Facilitate means to:

- *Make easy*
- *Make possible*
- *Smooth the progress of*
- *Help, aid, assist*

So, as the leader, you can decide what style your leadership will take in order to facilitate action. You may decide to facilitate the meeting yourself, or turn it over to someone else to facilitate and then become a participant. There may also be times when it is appropriate to hand it over to someone else to lead certain parts of the meeting, whilst you lead other parts. How do you make these decisions? You will need to consider a number of factors. For example . . .

Is the Meeting purpose:	Who should lead the meeting? Considerations?
To develop future plans for the team?	• Do you have the most knowledge about issues that will impact the team's future? If so, would it be best for you to facilitate the meeting or have someone else facilitate? • Do you have access to information that team members may not? Who would be best to facilitate? • Do you need to demonstrate your leadership to build credibility with the team? If so, should you facilitate?
To solve immediate or pressing team problems?	• Is the problem a content one, i.e. an issue with one of the team's tasks or goals? If so, you may decide to facilitate or hand over the meeting to one of your team members who is more closely involved with the task. • Is the problem a process one, e.g. something to do with team relationships? If so, it is most appropriate that you facilitate the meeting. Internal team processes are definitely your responsibility and nobody else's. • Would this be an opportunity to develop one of your team member's ability to facilitate the meeting?
To develop the skill, knowledge or competence of team members?	• Would this be an opportunity to develop one of your team member's ability to facilitate meetings? • Is there a team member who is an expert or knowledgeable on the topic? Should he/she facilitate the meeting?

Whether your meeting is to develop team plans, solve content or process issues, or develop the competence of team members, the following guidelines will ensure that your meeting remains focused and is productive. Keep in mind that if you decide to hand over the facilitation of the meeting to someone else, they may need your coaching on how to implement these facilitation guidelines.

There are six actions that you will need to take to ensure your problem solving meetings are successful:

1. Issue meeting pre-work
2. Agree ground rules for the session
3. Involve people in the discussion very early in the session
4. Use questions to stimulate discussion
5. Paraphrase and summarise the group's progress often
6. Encourage team members to take responsibility for results

1. Issue meeting pre-work – "start the meeting before the meeting"

Get each team member thinking about the topic before they get to the meeting. This not only allows everyone to think about the topic, it will also help bring out everyone's best thoughts and ideas.

Ask each participant to prepare for the meeting a few days in advance (one week is ideal, but not always possible) by jotting down some notes in answer to a short "meeting pre-work question". They need to bring these notes to the meeting.

The meeting pre-work question must be framed on the assumption that the problem has already been solved – i.e. it must be expressed at some future time. Following are examples of pre-work questions for three different types of problem solving meetings. Change and adapt these to suit your meeting needs.

What To Do When You Become The Boss

How to frame pre-work questions for meetings to solve *CONTENT* or *PROCESS* issues:

For example, if a telephone service department were looking for ideas on how they could improve their service, the question might be put:

"Assume that we have just had a very successful year, and that we have received heaps of positive feedback which suggested our service given to customers has been first rate over the last twelve months:

- *What things did we do to get such great success?*

- *What problems or challenges did we have?*

- *How did we solve these problems or meet these challenges?"*

How to frame pre-work questions for meetings to decide on *FUTURE PLANS* for the team:

For meetings involving the development of future team plans, a similar pre-work question can be framed. For example:

"Assume that it is now 2010. Three years ago we sat down to work out a strategic plan for our team. Whilst we had to make some changes along the way, the plan worked really well. At the time we identified the strengths and weaknesses of the team as well as the opportunities the next three years would present for us. We also identified some of the things that might work against our plan being successful.

- *What team strengths did we use and develop to make our plan over the last 3 years so successful?*

- *What team weaknesses did we identify? How did we overcome these?*

- *What opportunities did we see for the team and how did we make the most of these?*

- *What threats to team success did we identify. What strategies did we put in place to ensure we successfully managed these possible threats?*

- *How did we identify when changes were needed to the plan over the 12 months? How did we make these changes?"*

How to frame pre-work questions for *TRAINING / DEVELOPMENT* meetings:

For training and development meetings, you could adapt the following pre-work question to meet your needs (Note; this sample meeting is being run in August):

"Assume It's now November. Back in August we ran a training and development meeting to bring everyone up to speed on the new XYZ system. Pete ran the meeting as he was our in-house expert.

- *What did each of us do to help make the session a success?*

- *What did I do to help Pete run the session successfully?*

- *How did we agree what our measure of success would be?"*

Of course training and development sessions may need more input from the "experts" – those people who are already competent in the area in which you want other team members to develop. Certainly the more skill that has to be passed on to the team members, the more directive the facilitation will need to be. However, always starting with a pre-work question similar to the above, will give the facilitator a flying start.

2. Agree ground rules for the session

Let's assume that you are running the first of these problem solving meetings with your team. You are a new manager. You have never run one before. The members don't yet know you well and haven't been involved in a meeting like this before. You will need to discuss and agree the role of the facilitator, you. In future sessions, you may ask one or more of your team to facilitate a session, so this initial discussion about ground rules is important. For example, you could ask your people at the start of the meeting:

- "Think about some of the more enjoyable and rewarding meetings / training sessions you've been in.
- What did the facilitator / trainer do?
- What did the participants do?"

Ask people to quickly jot down their answers, then draw out the two or three things that you believe will be most important during the meeting for both:

- the facilitator's role and
- the participants' role.

Write these two lists up in view of everyone (use a flip chart preferably as you can keep the page for future meetings). Make sure you stick to your facilitator ground rules during the session. When people get off the track, refer to the flipchart to remind them of the ground rules they developed and agreed to.

Keep your list of ground rules for future meetings. At the start of these meetings you can then confirm whether everyone is still in agreement with them, or they would like changes.

You can start to see why ground rules are so important. For example, running a ground rules discussion at the start of the meeting has already had the team make a decision before you have really got into what the meeting is all about. In fact they are a very good example of process management, which is the foundation for running effective meetings. More on process management towards the end of this chapter.

3. Involve people in the discussion very early in the session

Avoid a long introduction, just a brief intro, then straight into the ground rules. Make sure that everyone has the chance to participate early in the meeting. You will find that the extroverts take the early running, so it is important to include those of a more introverted nature as soon as possible. One of the ways of doing this is to direct a question to a quieter member. For example you could say; "Can you give me one of the ideas you had written down in answer to our pre-work question, Ray?"

Three more ideas for starting the meeting and involving people:

- For maximum participation, start the discussion or activity in pairs or small groups, then move the discussion/feedback to the main group. This becomes even more important if your team is a large one as it encourages participation from everyone very early in the session. For example you could ask people to discuss their answers to the pre-work question in small groups and come back to the main group in five minutes with the three most relevant points.

- At the meeting ask all participants for their ideas and list these on a whiteboard or flipchart paper. Note. It is very important to list these ideas so that everyone can see them – this helps maintain people's interest, keeps people focused and is useful for keeping the meeting on track.

- Not everybody is vocal and articulate enough to explain their thoughts off the cuff. Pre-work helps these people – tell all participants to start their contribution by reading their answers to the pre-work question. Then you can help the less vocal members by asking them to expand upon particular points. (This has another good effect – it forces you to listen well so that you can ask encouraging questions.)

4. Use questions to stimulate discussion

You should prepare these in advance. I always suggest that you prepare 15 possible discussion questions that you could ask. Why 15? There's no science or research to the number 15, just that I know through experience that not only will you have some great questions to ask, but in the process you'll probably also develop the answers to any question you might be asked! Remember, you will be facilitating this meeting, so it is likely that there will be a lot of discussion with plenty of questions from the team members.

In addition to your prepared questions, there are some standard questions and phrases that you should become familiar with. These will help people participate more fully and make the information being discussed much richer. Select and adapt some of the following to suit your own style. Use these regularly in all your meetings.

Facilitation Questions and phrases to stimulate discussion:

To encourage further discussion ...	To draw other people into the discussion ...
• *Tell me what you think about X...* • *Tell me more about...* • *Keep talking. Say more please.* • *Give me an example... or, For instance?* • *Explain to me...* • *Just say anything that comes to mind – everything's acceptable* • *Can you give me another item that you had listed on your pre-meeting worksheet?*	• *That's helpful. Let's hear some other views...* • *Let's hear a different perspective on that...* • *Who can add to that?* • *Does everyone accept that...?*
To help summarise key points or before moving to the next question ...	**To clarify the importance of a number of points that may have been raised ...**
• *If I've understood correctly, you mean...* • *So it sounds like you're saying...* • *So the message you want me to get from that example / story is...* • *So it's fair to say / conclude that...* • *In relation to this item, where are we at the moment?* • *Let me summarise what has been agreed so far ... Is everyone in agreement with that?*	• *Of all of the points that have been listed in answer to this question, which do you consider to be most important?* • *Can we rank these in order of importance?* • *Which would you consider to be the least important?* • *Sometimes it's a good idea to get participants to do the above (ranking) privately and then give their answers so as not to be influenced by others.* • *You could also get them to list the top 3 in order of importance or priority.*

5. Paraphrase and summarise the group's progress often - post discussion results in full view

This is important to keep the session on track. It is another example of good process management.

List the agreed points on flipchart paper progressively throughout the session. Place these in full view around the room. This provides a focus; a way of summarising; a sign that action is happening. It is also very helpful for you as the facilitator to refer back to from time to time to remind people what has been covered or to emphasise important points that they have already agreed on.

6. Encourage team members to take responsibility for results

When the meeting has reached agreement on which items are worthwhile and achievable:

- Make sure these are listed on flip chart paper in summary form.
- Add two further columns to each flip chart page. One column is headed "By when" and the other is headed "By whom". It is important that the workload for implementing the decisions is shared by all participants.
- In the first column "By when", ask the group to allocate a time for when this aspect could be achieved. When this is agreed, ask your people to volunteer to undertake responsibility for ensuring particular items are undertaken (not necessarily to do them, but to take responsibility for them), by placing their name in the "By whom" column.
- Once this is done, the meeting now has an action plan for solving the problem. This should be written up and distributed to people immediately following the meeting.

Note: Beware of 'Upward Delegation'. All the good books talk about delegating from the boss to others in the team. Problem solving meetings give the others a chance to get even. Given the opportunity, your people may put your name in the 'By Whom' column for every item.

If you are the leader of a team running a problem-solving meeting, and you find your name in the 'By Whom' column for the first three items on the list, there is a standard statement you must make: "OK, I'll accept those three, but no more. If you have any others you want to put my name against, somebody else will have to take accountability for one of these three."

Problem Solving Meetings – a Summary

Problem solving meetings are such an important part of the leadership element of your managerial role, that it's worthwhile highlighting some of the key points to follow to ensure your meeting is successful:

- Work as a facilitator not "the Boss"! Encourage open, positive, critical discussion. Putting on the boss' hat and making decisions about what can and cannot be done, soon stifles discussion and enthusiasm. On the other hand, being open and receptive, although difficult at times, will make the session stimulating and rewarding.
- It's very important to let your team know the decision making process for this session. For example, will you be making the decision after discussing the issue with the team, or will decisions they come up with be accepted by you?
- Assuming that you want to make this a motivational session, it is particularly important to accept all views - you don't have to agree with them, but you do have to accept them for discussion. Avoid putting the counter argument by using words such as "But ..." and "Yes, but ..." Instead ask "How might that work in practise?". Using "But" or "Yes, but ..." forces you into your boss' role. Asking "How might that work in practise?" shows you as a true facilitator.

Above all, by following the guidelines for problem solving meetings, you will find that you now have a committed team rather than a compliant one and that's truly motivational.

And now, process management

"Content" and "Process" have been mentioned a number of times in this chapter. Hopefully, through some of the examples given, you are starting to develop an understanding of the difference between the two and in particular, the importance of good process management.

- **Content is the "what" of the team meeting or session**

All groups and teams spend the majority of their time on getting the job done – these are the subjects they are discussing, the problems they are solving, the projects they are completing and so on. All of these can be referred to as "content". Content is all to do with task goals and objectives – the important work the team needs to do.

- **Process is the "how" the team works together**

Often, very little time is spent on assessing, monitoring or evaluating how effectively the group or team is working together to achieve the task. These activities, when carried out, are known as "process".

Teams that regularly spend time managing their process, perform better over the long term. Why? Teams that are good process managers are good:

- time keepers
- at giving one another feedback
- at involving everyone
- at taking account of individual differences
- at summarising and evaluating the progress they are making
- at sharing and taking leadership when it is needed
- at separating content from process
- at identifying and labelling key issues
- at managing conflict
- decision makers
- at gaining commitment to group decisions

Read the above list again. As a new manager, you would probably agree that learning to be a good process manager is one of the most important skills to develop. At the end of this chapter there's an activity, the Team Process Evaluation (TPE) to use regularly with your team meetings. You will find the TPE is a great tool for enhancing the process skills of both you and your team members.

HOW TO IMPLEMENT THE IDEAS IN THIS CHAPTER

☞ **How to start making your meetings more productive straight away**

- Decide whether your intended meeting is information sharing or problem solving
- Clearly identify what you want to achieve as an outcome from the meeting. e.g. Decisions? List of options? List of pros and cons? Commitment to a plan of action? Other?
- Use the 80/20 rule for all meetings – spend 80% of the meeting time focusing on the future and a maximum of 20% on the past

Things to do in your meetings	Reminder points and how to apply them
1. Get people involved in the topic before the session	• Issue pre-work in the form of a question • Make the question future oriented • Frame the question as if the problem has already been solved
2. Agree ground rules for the session	• Display these on flip chart paper
3. Involve people in the discussion very early in the session	• Ask questions • Refer people to their pre-work answers
4. Start the discussion in pairs or small groups	• Split group into smaller groups
5. Use questions to stimulate discussion.	• Prepare 15 possible questions
6. Involve all team members	• Ask questions of quieter members • Appoint leaders of sub groups
7. Paraphrase and summarise the group's progress often	• List summary points on flipchart paper throughout the session
8. Post discussion results in full view	• List or highlight agreed points on flipchart paper
9. Encourage team members to take responsibility for results	• Assign roles, e.g. penciller, note taker • Ask people to select items they can

	take control of
10. **Ensure there is an "Action" at the end of the session**	• List action points together with who has the responsibility for their completion, plus time lines and follow-up actions
11. **Encourage open, positive, critical discussion**	• Listen • Avoid use of "But" and "Yes, but" • Take off your boss' hat

☞ **How to make your meetings and training sessions fully productive and motivational**

Part A: **Use the following checklist to plan and conduct your meetings.**

Things to Consider . . .	Questions to answer . . .
Phase 1: Analyse the meeting tasks and the topic	
Is the meeting information sharing or problem solving?	• Is there a real need for the meeting? Could it be handled in another way?
Objectives for you	• What do you want to walk away with? Decisions? List of options? List of pros and cons? Commitment to a plan of action? Other?
Objectives for your people	• What do the participants want?
What are the limits or constraints?	• Time? Authority? Resources - People? Finance? Materials? • Do you need to set a start and finish time?
What aspects of the topic can the group reasonably cover?	• Do you need to form sub-groups? Involve experts?
Location for the meeting	• Is the location suitable? • Comfortable? • Creating the appropriate mood? • Should it be held in the workplace or off-site? • What equipment will be needed?
Create and distribute an agenda	• List major items. Set times. • List who will attend. What the meeting

	will accomplish. When and where it will be held. Why they need to come. • Is pre-meeting work appropriate? • How much notice do people need of the meeting?
Phase 2: Identify participants and their likely needs	
Who will be responsible for implementation?	• How will you ensure this happens?
Who should attend the meeting?	• Who can add value? • Who will be the greatest supporter? • Who will be the greatest opponent? • Who is likely to cause conflict?
Can the group make decisions or only recommendations?	• Who will be able to make decisions? • How will you let the group know?
Participation at the meeting	• Do people need to interact? • Ask questions? • Give/seek feedback? • Confirm opinions?
Phase 3: Conduct or facilitate the meeting	
Meeting leadership	• Who will conduct or facilitate the meeting? • How will you ensure it stays on track?
Participation during the meeting	• How will you involve everyone? • How will you ensure that everyone has a say and is listened to?
Disagreement and conflict	• How will you manage disagreement and conflict should they arise?
Decisions and commitment	• How will you ensure people are committed to the decisions made?
Evaluating progress	• How will you keep time? • How will you summarise progress?

Part B: Use the following Team Process Evaluation regularly

1. Spend 5 - 10 minutes at the end of every team meeting evaluating how well the team managed the process issues. List "Review of Team Process" as the last agenda item. The first time you use this, it will probably take 15 to 20 minutes as people will need time to familiarise themselves with the process.

2. Once you have run the first meeting to demonstrate, give someone else the responsibility for chairing the 5-minute segment for your next meeting. This can be rotated from meeting to meeting.

3. Ask all team members to individually score the five process measures and list their three adjectives without any discussion. This should be done in silence.

4. Discuss ratings and particularly differences.

   • Encourage people to give examples from the meeting that explain their ratings. *What can we learn for next meeting? What do we need to do differently? How can we manage our meetings better?*

   • Note: There is no need to reach consensus on the ratings – they are merely to guide the discussion and to encourage the sharing of feedback. Try to avoid discussion on the scores per se. Also be very careful not to get back into the content of the meeting – this agenda item is about process management, not content. Sometimes people will want to discuss the content, particularly if they were less than happy with the outcome during the meeting. Content issues can wait till next meeting or be discussed outside of this meeting – the time now is to discuss process only.

5. Finish with a brief sharing of the three adjectives to gather the mood of the meeting. This can reinforce or sometimes highlight an issue that didn't come up in the discussion of the five process measures. Often people only express their feelings when they use an adjective to describe the mood of the meeting.

Note: When using this process management technique for the first time, you may need to spend some time discussing the difference between process and content. To start with, it is recommended that you use this during every meeting – do this for at least the first month, then after that you can use the process every three to four weeks.

Team Process Evaluation

To be completed <u>individually</u>, in <u>silence</u>, by each team member and then discussed by the entire team. The aim is to discuss process improvement, not to reach consensus on the scores.

Direction and Leadership			*RATING*					
● How much direction and leadership was displayed during the meeting?	None	1	2	3	4	5	A great deal
Participation								
● How understood and listened to, did you feel?	Not at all	1	2	3	4	5	Completely
● How satisfied are you with the amount and quality of your participation in your team's decision making?	Dissatisfied	1	2	3	4	5	Completely satisfied
Disagreement and Conflict								
● How effectively was disagreement and conflict handled?	Not well	1	2	3	4	5	Very positively
Decisions and Commitment								
● How much influence did you feel you had on the decisions?	Very little	1	2	3	4	5	A great deal
● How committed are you to the decision(s) your team made?	Uncommitted	1	2	3	4	5	Very committed
● How much responsibility will you take for making the decision work?	Very little	1	2	3	4	5	Full responsibility
Evaluating Progress								
● How effectively was the team's gress evaluated during the meetin	Not at all	1	2	3	4	5	Consistently
● How effectively were process is handled during the meeting?	Not at all	1	2	3	4	5	Completely

Part 5: Managing Yourself

How do you get the best out of yourself?

W hen I first started to write this book, I debated whether to put this section up the front. For example Chapter 16 "How to manage yourself" is principally concerned with things such as "life / work balance", "time management" and "managing stress". In fact the first sub heading in that chapter is "A good starting point for the new manager".

So, what changed my mind? Why isn't this part of the book one of the first you should read? Well, it contains all the good stuff and advice that we know we should do or take, but often don't. My logic in putting it last is that by now I am hopeful that you have implemented some of the suggestions made earlier in the book and seen that they actually work. Hence, you may now be more motivated to follow some of the advice in Part 5. That's my thinking. It's now over to you for the application.

I'm not going to provide any learning tips for Part 5. I believe you should dive in where you think you can get the most advantage. Part 5 contains:

- Chapter 16: How to manage yourself
- Chapter 17: How to delegate
- Chapter 18: How to become more productive
- Chapter 19: How to manage your email
- Chapter 20: Five of the worst mistakes new managers make and five principles on how to avoid them
- Chapter 21: How to develop yourself to your full potential
- Chapter 22: How to develop your image, your persona

All the best for the further development of your managerial career.

Bob Selden

Chapter 16

How to Manage Yourself

A good starting point for the New Manager

This is one of the hardest chapters I have had to write. I've written much on how to manage – others. But managing oneself is a bit different. Why? Each one of us is a different and unique individual. We all approach life in our own individual manner.

So, are there any general principles that perhaps apply to everyone of us?

Yes, fortunately there are. More of that in a moment. But first, let me explain the reason for this Chapter. When I started writing this book I had really not considered "self management" as a topic. Then a friend of mine, Colin, convinced me how important the topic is for new managers.

Colin was about to become a new manager. He asked me what he should do when taking over his new role. Having watched many new managers over the years and trained quite a few, I have seen how challenging the new manager's role can be.

I also remember very clearly from my own experience as a new manager, what it was like. One day you are a technical or professional expert where you know most of the answers and how to really problem-solve. Next day you move to being an expert people manager. Well, that's what most of the people around you expect you to be – and generally straight away!

Colin was concerned because the previous person in his new role had not been very successful as a people manager. As one of the brightest technical people in the organisation, big things were expected of Colin.

All eyes were upon him.

Here's the advice I gave to Colin. As a new manager, it may also be useful for you.

1. Monitor your work hours

- **Set a limit and stick to it.**

It's very easy to get sucked into working longer and longer hours just because you are new to the role and have so much to learn. The law of diminishing returns starts to kick in after a certain period of time at work each day, i.e. the longer you work, the less you actually achieve. Far better to work more effectively in less hours. Be particularly careful if you hear yourself saying things like "Well, I'm only new to the role, so it's probably expected that I should take longer".

- **Plan the order in which you do things every day.**

For example, most people think that doing their emails first thing in the morning is a good use of time – get them out of the way so that you can get on with the job. Wrong!

Research suggests that for two thirds of us, the morning is the most creative time. If you are amongst this group, then wasting good creative time on a mundane task such as emails, means you will be less effective over the long term. When you finally get through all those emails each morning, your creativity for problem solving and decision making has evaporated. It's also a well known fact that for most people immediately after lunch is the least productive time of the day. This is the best time therefore to tackle the emails.

2. Recognise and manage your signs of stress

Each of us has a different reaction to stress. Unfortunately, when we are stressed, we often don't realise it until it becomes too late and we get ill or it severely affects our performance.

There are four things that will help you identify when you are stressed; your:

- thoughts,
- actions,
- physical symptoms and
- emotions.

- Are your thoughts more negative than usual? e.g. "I can't cope" or, Are you recalling and focusing on recent failures rather than all the things you have done well lately?
- Are your actions somewhat different? e.g. Avoiding things you should be doing, or lack of coordination?
- Is your body responding differently to pressure? e.g. A racing heart, rapid breathing or sweating more than usual? For some people other bodily symptoms such as an outbreak of acne or sudden increase in dandruff, can also mean an onset of stress.
- Have your feelings changed lately? e.g. Do you feel panic, anger, irritable, scared more easily?

Sometimes it's hard for us to recognize our own symptoms. So to help recognize some of these symptoms, it may be useful to get some outside help. Find someone who knows you well and ask them to give you feedback at least every two weeks on how you seem to be coping in your new role.

If you are starting to show some of these signs of stress, then you need to take some action. Look to find more of a balance between:

- intellectual,
- physical and
- emotional activities.

There are some pointers on how to do this later in this chapter.

3. Learn to delegate

Failure to delegate is the most common mistake new managers make. For managers, there are two key aspects to successful delegation:

- Having people to whom one can delegate, and
- Selecting the most appropriate tasks to delegate

The key to delegation is to develop within your people, the "initiative to take action" so that they learn to develop their skills and knowledge to their full potential.

How do you do this? When your people have a problem that they want some help with, encourage them to come to you with their recommended solutions, not just the problem. If they do not have any solutions, make sure that they at least come to you with a plan of action for finding a solution (which by the way, should not be based around asking you).

Secondly, draw up a list of things that you could delegate, then decide who best to delegate them to. Who's ready? Who needs further development?

Delegation is so important, that there is an entire chapter on some of the details of how to delegate (Chapter 17).

4. Communicate, communicate, communicate!

This means regular meetings with:

- your team members
- your boss.

It also means talking over work issues with a partner, friend or trusted colleague (from another area) on a regular basis to give you some feedback on how well you are communicating.

At a very basic level, this also means responding to emails on the same day. If you can't answer an email fully, then send a response to say that it has been received. One of the criteria on which every manager is judged, is their ability and willingness to communicate. Rightly or wrongly, one of the criteria people will judge you on is your responsiveness to emails (sometimes even more so than their content).

5. Give praise and recognition regularly

Even a "Thank You" is important. Look for the things people are doing well and praise them. If appropriate for the person, also give public recognition. Of all the motivational tools you have at your disposal, this is by far the easiest and cheapest, yet brings the biggest payoffs.

Yet, there is an even more important payoff for you personally when you give praise – it makes you feel good. Try it now.

6. Focus on what is important, not what is urgent

In particular, talk with your manager about the three most important priorities he/she has for you in your role. Make sure you focus on these at all times.

A simple way of doing this, is to have a discussion with him or her, preferably soon after you start in the role. Ask your manager;

- "What are the top three priorities in the role that you would like me to focus on?"

Or, if you have a formal performance discussion,

- Ask your manager to assign a percentage figure of "importance" against each one of your key responsibility areas so that you can assess his or her priorities. Each key responsibility should be given a percentage out of a total for all areas of 100%, or if you like, points out of 100. You should also ask when discussing each responsibility "Why is this so important?" The answer will give you a host of good clues for developing the relationship with your manager. These clues are most likely your boss' unwritten expectations.

If you need some more information on how to do this, it is covered in detail in Chapter 12 "How to manage your boss" .

7. Ensure you have a balance between intellectual, physical and emotional activities

Whilst people differ markedly in their biorhythms (the way we manage our mental, physical and emotional makeup), each of us needs to manage these three. Of all the points raised so far on self management, this is probably the most important.

Successful sports people are really good self-management role models for us because we can see their results very quickly on the sporting field. From my own work in sports psychology, I know that athletes who are successful are particularly good at maintaining a balance between mental, physical and emotional activities. My work with managers over many years shows that the same is true for effective managers, particularly new managers.

What does this mean for the new manager?

Implementing action in relation to the previous six self-management steps is a good start – if you look back at them you will see they in fact cover a range of mental, physical and emotional activities. In addition, you should consider:

- **Intellectual**. Regularly undertake a mind activity such as reading a good book, seeing a movie, learning a new language or starting a creative hobby such as painting. Keep in mind that this needs to be regular, not spasmodic.
- **Physical**: Ensure that you have an exercise regime that keeps you physically fit. This doesn't have to be strenuous, but it does have to challenge you. Also watch your diet. Once again the regular regime is important, not fits and starts.
- **Emotional:** Take care to interact regularly with the special people in your life – make time for them. I've often heard managers say to a loved one "I can't make it this weekend, but when this project is over, I'll make it up to you". Trust me. You never do. You can never make up lost loved-one time. I know in my own case, I can clearly remember the family events I have missed over the years, but I cannot remember the important work issue or project that caused me to miss the event. Have you missed any of these family events already?

Also think about building new relationships with people outside work. While it's nice to have a range of friends at work, it's also important to have people with whom you can discuss subjects other than work.

Finally, find yourself a mentor

This should be someone who has been or is a successful people manager.

Without exception, the most successful managers I have met tell me that they have someone that they often confide in or whose help they seek when faced with a new challenge.

Meet regularly with your mentor to discuss your issues, challenges and ways that you can learn and develop. Don't expect a mentor to have all the answers, but they can be very useful as a sounding board to bounce ideas off. Speaking from personal experience as a manager and consultant for over 30 years, I still call on my mentor Dennis from time to time for his advice.

I'm now really pleased that Collin asked his question of me which led to me struggling over writing this chapter. In the process, I actually had to stretch my intellectual capacity. For me, I'm now off to do some physical exercise on the bike and then later this evening to have a relaxing dinner with my wife.

Enjoy your life – It's the only one you will have!

HOW TO IMPLEMENT THE IDEAS IN THIS CHAPTER

 How to start Managing Yourself straight away

1. Monitor your work hours	<ul><li>Set a time for finishing work each day and stick to it.</li><li>Listen to the self-voice that says "I'm only new so I have to work longer". Ignore it. Stick to your established finishing time.</li><li>Do your creative tasks early in the day and your boring ones (e.g. emails) straight after lunch.</li></ul>

2. **Recognise and manager your signs of stress**	• Are your thoughts more negative than usual? e.g. "I can't cope" or "I always get this wrong". • Are your actions somewhat different? e.g. Avoiding things you should be doing, or lack of coordination? • Is your body responding differently to pressure? e.g. A racing heart, rapid breathing or sweating more than usual? • Have your feelings changed lately? e.g. Do you feel panic, anger, irritable, scared more easily? • Ask a friend to help monitor your signs.
3. **Learn to delegate**	• Work out who you can delegate to. • Identify what you can delegate. • Train and coach your people to take more initiative.
4. **Communicate, communicate, communicate!**	• Have regular meetings (weekly) with your boss; your team. • Respond to your emails on the same day.
5. **Give praise and recognition regularly**	• On a daily basis, look for people who are doing things well and personally "thank them".
6. **Focus on what is important, not what is urgent**	• Make sure you know the key priorities your manager has set for you (written and unwritten).
7. **Ensure you have a balance between intellectual, physical and emotional activities**	• Undertake a mind activity regularly – something outside of work to stretch your brain muscles either intellectually and / or creatively. • Develop and stick to a regular exercise regime. Watch your diet. • Spend quality time with your loved ones and friends.
8. **Find yourself a mentor**	• Find someone who will take an interest in your success as a manager. • Ask for his / her advice regularly.

Chapter 17

How to Delegate

In Chapter Two, we described a manager as somebody who:

- gets things done
- through other people

You can get things done through other people by telling them step by step what to do. Or, you can tell them the results you require them to achieve and delegate to them the authority to make the decisions which will achieve those results.

Delegation always includes decision making

Delegation is something you do with "authority to decide" – you give people decision making authority. You delegate "authority to make decisions" that may or may not achieve a set of required results. The decisions may be quite minor, or they could be quite major. It's not just something you do with a task, which is the old "command and control" principle of telling people what to do.

Delegation always involves trust

You have to trust other people's judgment if you are going to delegate authority to them. Many managers (particularly new managers) believe that their judgment is better than everybody else's, so it is more comfortable to make the decision and tell others what to do rather than to delegate the decision-authority to others.

The Achilles heel of new managers – absence of delegating

How come you've worked hard all day but haven't started the one task that was most important to you? As a manager, how come your daily work schedule often falls in a heap by mid-morning?

In their very famous article "Management Time: Who's got the Monkey?", (Harvard Business Review, Nov. 1999), Oncken and Wass suggested that there are three types of management-imposed time pressure:

- Boss,
- System, and
- Self.

• Boss-imposed time pressure

Activities imposed by your boss, which must be accomplished or you'll suffer the consequences.

• System-imposed time pressure

Those activities/requests which come from peers and colleagues. The penalties are not so severe or as swift as those imposed by your boss, but you may still suffer if these things are not done.

• Self-imposed time pressure

Those activities you initiate or choose to do – particularly those things which have been upwardly delegated from people who report to you. As managers, these activities impact heavily on your discretionary time. The penalty for not doing these is stress.

Oncken and Wass used the analogy of the "monkey on your back" to make their point. As the manager, when someone in your team talks about a problem they want to "run past you", the monkey (in other words, the problem) is very clearly on their back. But when you respond with something like "Well, I haven't got time right now, but leave it with me", the monkey immediately leaps from their shoulders to yours. You have just been on the receiving end of an excellent piece of upward delegation. (All the good books on managing talk about delegating downward. They rarely mention the cleverness with which people delegate upward.)

If this happens to you every day, or at least more often than it should, you'll soon be carrying a cage full of monkeys on your back. Not only have you reduced your discretionary time, you also must now feed and care for the monkeys you've acquired. For example, your people are probably pretty good at keeping track of their upwardly delegated task, when they say things like "Hey boss, how's that issue going that I told you about the other day?"

How do you avoid having monkeys dumped on your back by others and give yourself more discretionary time? The first step is to recognise that the monkeys are jumping onto your back!

Use the following checklist to see whether you are a collector of monkeys. Answer each with "Always", "Often" or "Rarely".

How often do I say?	Always ☐	Often ☐	Rarely ☐
"Leave it with me"			
"Can I think about that?"			
"I'll get back to you on that"			
"I've seen something like that a thousand times before. I'll look after it for you"			
"I'll get Bob to look after that"			
"Send me an e-mail on that will you?"			
"Don't you worry about it"			

If you found yourself answering "Always" or "Often" for most or many of these, **then it's probably too late. The monkey has just jumped!** There's a very good chance that you are taking on the problems of your people, rather than helping them solve the problems themselves. In the process, you've reduced your discretionary time and they have lost a good opportunity to develop their own skills and knowledge.

Like to try again? Use the same "Always", "Often" or "Rarely" on the following questions.

How often do I say?	Always ☐	Often ☐	Rarely ☐
"Let me know if you have trouble"			
"You know you don't have to do it that way"			
"That's interesting. I've never seen any- thing quite like that before"			
"I remember when that happened to . . . "			
"I think my last boss had something like that happen to him/her"			

If you found yourself answering "Always" or "Often", then the result is not as bad as the result would be from the first list. **However, beware! The monkey is about to jump.** While the responses sound very suppor-tive and helpful (which they are), starting out like this invariably ends up with you, the manager taking on the problem to solve. It's the first step in accepting upward delegation.

How did you score on both lists of questions? Do you use similar phrases to some of the ones in the checklists? If you found yourself ticking a number of "always" or "often" columns, or you use similar phrases regu-larly, then chances are you need to be careful about taking on too many monkeys.

The difference between what you *can do* and what you *should do*

To start the delegation process, you need to think about:

– what you **should** and **can** do, then
– what **others** could do for you.

What you *should do* is about setting your priorities and sticking with them:

• What are the two or three things that you must achieve today, come what may?

223

- Do not be swayed from these.

What you *can do* has nothing to do with your ability. Rather it is about the amount of time you have available and how you use that time – in other words, your discretionary time. As the manager, you are the expert – your people know that there are lots of things that you can do. Do not be trapped into doing things just because you know how. While it may take a little bit of your time to teach or coach someone else, in the long run doing so will save you heaps of time.

The secret to successful delegation - developing the *ability to take initiative* within your people

The secret is to reduce the pressure of self-imposed activities to give you more discretionary time. You can then use this time to become more productive with your boss and the system and in the process, a better manager.

What "others can do for you" is about your willingness and ability to delegate. Developing your people to take responsibility will provide you with more discretionary time to devote to other activities.

There are two aspects to successful delegation:

- Having **people** to whom one can delegate, and
- Selecting the most **appropriate tasks** to delegate authority for

The key to delegation is to develop within your people, the
"initiative to take action"
so that they learn to develop their skills and knowledge to their full potential.

This is so pivotal to effective delegation that it's worth repeating:

The key to delegation is to develop within your people, the
"initiative to take action"
so that they learn to develop their skills and knowledge to their full potential.

Managers who are successful are always good at delegating. Less successful managers, when asked why they don't delegate more, often respond:

- *"If only my staff were more experienced" or,*
- *"I don't have enough faith in my staff to do the job properly" or,*
- *"Delegation. Sounds great in theory, but I need to have fully trained staff and I don't have the time to train them" or,*
- *"By the time I have explained what I want, I might as well have done it myself".*

If some of these comments sound familiar to you, then the following steps will show you how to:

- Identify the current *level of initiative* of each of your team members.
- Use the *level of initiative ranking* (follows at the end of this chapter) with your team to further develop their skills and knowledge.

The five levels of initiative

When delegating, it is important to fit the task to the person and to ensure the reason for delegating is appropriate.

Is it possible to delegate to all your team members? The answer is "Yes" and "No", as the following table will clarify.

Level	For delegation purposes, team members may be classified as those who ...
1.	Wait until he or she is told what to do.
2.	Do what is necessary, but refer to you all problems or slightly unusual issues for a decision.
3.	Refer all problems or unusual occurrences for a decision to you, but when doing so recommend appropriate action.
4.	Take action on problems as they occur and then immediately report on the action taken.
5.	Take action on all issues and problems on their own initiative and then report periodically on progress.

Which level should your team members reach?

Managers who are less successful, unknowingly keep their team members at the second level, i.e.

- Do what is necessary, but refer to their supervisor all problems or slightly unusual issues for a decision, by not encouraging them to make recommendations on problems or issues they encounter. As a consequence, their people rarely develop the knowledge or skills they need to become fully competent.

Successful managers quickly move all their people through to at least level three, i.e.

- Refer all problems or unusual occurrences for a decision, but when doing so recommend appropriate action.

When people are at level three, they are always looking for solutions rather than just stating the problem. Not only do they look for solutions, but when they do bring a problem to you, they bring their recommended solution as well. Wouldn't your life as a manager be so much easier if all your people did this?

Successful managers then move individual staff from level three through levels four and five depending on the particular team member's skill and how quickly they can gain the necessary experience.

Training people to take initiative

Many successful managers take this one step further. They use the *levels of initiative* as a training tool by involving their team members in the process of developing initiative. For instance, they explain the five-step level of initiative process to them and then ask:

- What level do you believe you are at now on each of your major job responsibilities?
- How can you move to the next level?

Using this approach, you can then be very clear about which aspects of a person's job the team member can take initiative on, and how much initiative they may take. It is also a great opportunity to talk about training and development strategies to help move people to the next level on particular job responsibilities. In this way, you know exactly who within your team, you can delegate certain tasks to and most importantly, how they will respond.

When the majority of your people are at level five, delegation becomes automatic. In fact, you will find that you won't have to delegate, your team will take the initiative.

Can all tasks be delegated?

The second aspect of delegation is to decide which tasks may be delegated.

Tasks suitable for delegation include:

- Minor and repetitive decisions.
- Tasks you are expert in and that others should learn.
- Tasks for which you are least qualified, but that others could learn.
- Tasks you dislike, provided someone else likes them (delegation should not be an excuse to dump unpleasant tasks).
- Tasks that add variety and interest to another person's role.
- Tasks that will increase the number of people who can perform critical assignments.

Which tasks could you delegate?

Remember, whatever you delegate still remain part of your job. While you can delegate responsibility and decision making authority for them, you always remain accountable for the total team output.

One of the questions often asked by managers is

- *"How do I keep track of what's been delegated?"*

If you use the levels of initiative protocol by discussing and agreeing each person's permitted level of initiative, you will note that levels 3,4 & 5 all have built in reporting mechanisms. Make sure you agree how these will operate with your people.

Following these guidelines will allow you to release some of your monkeys back to where they can be properly cared for and fed by others – your team members.

HOW TO IMPLEMENT THE IDEAS IN THIS CHAPTER

☞ **How to start delegating straight away**

- When one of your team member's comes to you with a problem that you think they should be able to solve, try using one of the following questions:
    - How do you think it would be best to handle this?
    - What ideas have you had that might help resolve this issue?
    - Is there a similar experience you have had in the past? How did you handle that one?
    - If I wasn't here to help on this, what would you do?
    - Who else have you spoken to about this? What were their thoughts? Which options do you think are best to apply here? Why?

- Decide on some tasks that you can delegate. Remember, these should be:
    - Minor and repetitive decisions.
    - Tasks you are expert in and that others should learn.
    - Tasks for which you are least qualified, but that others could learn.
    - Tasks you dislike, provided someone else likes them (delegation should not be an excuse to dump unpleasant tasks).
    - Tasks that add variety and interest to another person's role.
    - Tasks that will increase the number of people who can perform critical assignments.

- Give your team members this chapter to read. Tell them you would like everyone to:
    - Be at least at level three.
    - Tell you how they intend to develop their skills and knowledge

to their full potential so that they can be at level 5 on most tasks.

☞ **How to become an expert delegator by developing each team member's *level of initiative***

Four options here. Use the following "DEVELOPING INITIATIVE IN TEAM MEMBERS" grid for each option. Have a look at it now, before you read the options. You may need to amend the grid slightly for each option.

Option 1: Overall analysis of the level of initiative within your team
- List all of your team members across the top, one per column. If you have more than six team members, add the necessary columns.
- Think about each team member in turn.
- Tick the level you believe each team member is currently at for the majority of their responsibilities. If you find it too difficult to do this, perhaps because they are at different levels for different responsibilities, go straight to Option 2.
- Decide what development / training / coaching activities they need to move them to the next level.
- Draw up a development plan for each team member.
- Discuss and agree the plan with each team member.
- For those team members who are already at level 5, decide which of your tasks / duties you could delegate to them.
- Draw up and discuss a development plan for these team members as well. Even though they are at level 5, they will still respond to development.

Option 2: Analysis of the level of initiative of each of your team members
- Use a separate grid for each team member. Write their name at the top of each sheet.
- Think about each team member in turn. In the *Team Member" space, instead of people's names (Option 1), list the 5 or 6 major responsibilities for this particular team member across the top of the grid, one major responsibility per column.
- Tick the level you believe he/she is currently at for each of their re-

sponsibilities.

- Decide what development / training / coaching activities he/she may need to move them to the next level in each area of responsibility.
- Draw up a development plan for each team member.
- Discuss and agree the plan with each team member.
- For those team members who are already at level 5 on the majority of their responsibilities, decide which of your tasks / duties you could delegate to them.
- Draw up and discuss a development plan for these team members as well. Even though they are at level 5, they will still respond to development.

Option 3: Giving each team member responsibility for doing his/her own analysis of their level of initiative

- Give each team member a copy of this chapter to read or a copy of the original article "Who's Got The Monkey Now? How To Find Out How Well You Manage Your Time" (available at: http://www.nationallearning.com.au/index_files/HowToMakePeople FeelBetterAtWork.htm)
- Same as Options 1 & 2 with the exception that you hand the grid over to each team member to complete.
- This option is a great way to speed and enhance the development of initiative within your people.

Option 4: Giving the team the responsibility for assessing their level of initiative

- Similar to Option 3, only you do this as a whole team.
- Give each team member a copy of this chapter to read or a copy of the original article "Who's Got The Monkey Now? How To Find Out How Well You Manage Your Time" (available at: http://www.nationallearning.com.au/index_files/HowToMakePeople FeelBetterAtWork.htm)
- Run a team meeting around the chapter or article.
- Ask team members to discuss what level they think the team is at for the majority of their responsibilities.
- Ask team members to decide how they could move to the next level.
- Ask team members to decide which of your tasks they could do for you – what training / coaching / development would they need?

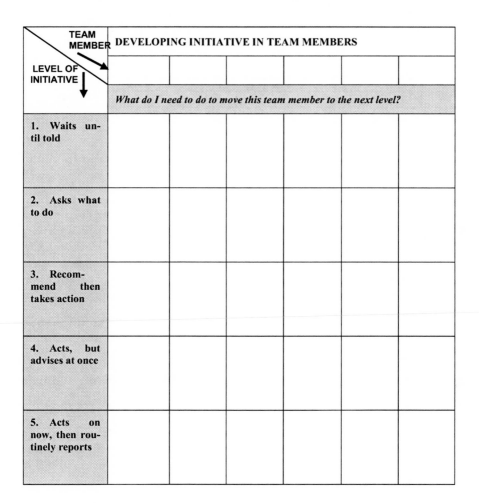

TEAM MEMBER / LEVEL OF INITIATIVE	DEVELOPING INITIATIVE IN TEAM MEMBERS					
	What do I need to do to move this team member to the next level?					
1. Waits until told						
2. Asks what to do						
3. Recommend then takes action						
4. Acts, but advises at once						
5. Acts on now, then routinely reports						

Chapter 18

How to Become More Productive

How Busy Are You?

You receive a phone call from the CEO who asks whether you'd be interested in taking on a special assignment. In this assignment you would report directly to the CEO and participate in making some of the important strategic decisions facing the organisation. This assignment would provide you personally with major growth and career opportunities. The offer has only one catch; because the assignment is only part time requiring about one day per week, you would have to do your present job in the remaining four days. Would you take the assignment?

Before reading any further please answer ""Yes" or "No" – *Would you take the assignment?*

Harvard Business Review (Ashkenas, R.N. and Schaffer R.H., Jan 2002) report that this question has been posed to hundreds of managers, most of whom believed that they already lacked the time to do their jobs properly. Yet, ninety nine percent of them take the assignment. Why?

Are these managers:

- Admitting that if the motivation were powerful enough, they could eliminate or do in much less time, eight to ten hours worth of current activities each week without negative consequences?
- Currently spending time performing unproductive, time wasting activities that they could easily drop, to avoid or escape job related anxiety?

Like the other 99% of managers, did you answer "Yes"?

If so, what activities that you currently do, could you eliminate or do less of to free up some of your time for the more important things you need to do? Or perhaps, get somebody else to do? Delegate?

Time management – fact or fiction?

As the HBR article points out, almost all managers escape some job-induced anxiety through a variety of unproductive, often unconscious, psychological mechanisms – rationalisation, denial, blaming and so forth. One of the most costly is busyness; the escape into time consuming activities that managers find less threatening to perform, though much less productive, than the tough aspects of their jobs.

These time consuming activities could be aptly named "comfort tasks" – comfort because they are generally mindless and easy to do. However, having done them, have we progressed any of the major tasks we need to achieve? The answer is almost certainly "No". But we have put off until a later time the things we know we have to do. Like good food, comfort tasks make us feel good, but if we have too much, we feel bloated. The trick is to keep the comfort tasks to an enjoyable minimum and thus not become time management obese.

Time management comfort food and the weight loss plan!

So, how do you reduce the amount of time spent on comfort tasks?

The first step is to become aware of how much time you actually spend on these comfort tasks. Remember, for most of us, these comfort tasks are done unconsciously, so we need to find out what they are.

Once you have identified your comfort tasks, make a conscious effort to reduce the amount of time you spend on them. Keep in mind, that some time spent is OK and healthy, but overdoing it is overdosing.

In the future, should you find your mind wandering, remember the "comfort task" trick and get back on track. This simple technique is bound to free up some of your time to focus on the really important things either within your job or private life.

How do you determine what is important?

Stephen Covey, who wrote the popular book "7 Habits of Highly Effective People" almost 20 years ago, introduced a "how to" matrix to help us identify what is important and distinguish the important from the urgent.

Urgent tasks are deadline based. These are usually independent of you and are often driven by others. The sooner the task needs completion the more urgent it is. Urgency does not necessarily relate to importance. Common urgent (but not necessarily important) tasks include answering emails, attending other people's meetings that have little bearing on your own effectiveness, completing some routine, regular reports that do not show any productive outcomes or results.

Important activities are those that help you achieve your goals. The importance of a task should determine how much time you want to spend on it. Notice that this is independent of urgency and is what you want or need to do, not what others want you to do. These important tasks will be specific to each of us, but some common important activities might include relationship building (particularly with loved ones, boss and team), planning a personal 12-month development strategy, attending a personal development workshop.

Stephen Covey's Time Management Matrix

Covey provides us with a neat way of categorizing urgent and importance tasks so that it is easy to make a decision whether to:

- Do it now
- Plan when to do it
- Put off till later
- Don't do it

His matrix plots an Urgency axis against an Importance axis and provides us with four quadrants into which we can plot the activities or tasks that constantly vie for our time.

	Urgent	Not Urgent
Important	**Quadrant 1** *Do now or suffer the consequences*	**Quadrant 2** *Prioritise and set a start date for each*
Not Important	**Quadrant 3** *Place these on your "to Do" list but after Quadrant 2 items*	**Quadrant 4** *Can be put off – only take action if they are likely to move to Q2 or Q3*

Adapted from Covey, Stephen R. The 7 Habits of Highly Effective People , Simon & Schuster, New York 1990

Sometimes it's hard to judge exactly which quadrant a particular task should fall into. The trick with a model such as Covey's Time Management Matrix, is to learn how to use it almost without thinking about it throughout the day. Try using it for one week every time you find yourself thinking "Should I be doing this now?" or "What do I do next, there seems so much to do?"

Here's a simple two step process to assist:

Step 1. Decide how important is the task. The first question to answer is:

- "Is this task important?"

When judging whether an item is important or not ask:

235

- "Will this activity move me toward my longer term goal?"

If your answer is "Yes", then it goes in either "Q1 Important & Urgent" or "Q2 Important but not Urgent."

If your answer is "No", then it goes in Q3 (do later, but put a date on it) or Q3 – put off, no need to worry.

Step 2: If important, do it now or prioritise. Because you have now defined the task as important, you need to decide:

- "Is it urgent, i.e., what will be the consequences of not doing this now? (Q1)" or
- "When will I commit to take the next action to move it forward (Q2, not urgent, but important)?" Make sure you diary this action straight away.

The real power of the Important vs. Urgent matrix is to recognise that we should always make sure that tasks which are important come before tasks which are urgent.

PS. I have found that many of my comfort food tasks fall into Q4. Food for thought?

HOW TO IMPLEMENT THE IDEAS IN THIS CHAPTER

☞ **How to start becoming more productive, straight away**

For the next week:

- Place a very bright post-it note somewhere visible with a large question: "Is this a comfort task?", so that you will see it regularly throughout the day.
- When you find your mind wandering or day dreaming, or you find yourself not working on the required major goals, tasks or activities, stop!
- Write down what you are physically doing right now – this is most

likely a comfort task.

- Take a note of these things you do that are comfort tasks, i.e. they are not progressing your major goals or activities.

- Keep a note of all your comfort tasks for the week.

During the following week:

- Make a conscious effort to reduce the amount of time you spend on identified comfort tasks. When you find yourself working on a comfort task, go straight back to your major goals or activities.

- Keep in mind, that some time spent on comfort tasks is OK and healthy. We all need a little comfort sometime. But overdoing it is overdosing!

 How to really become more productive

1. Draw up a list of the really important goals in your life – business and personal. Decide what action you are going to take over the next 12 months to progress these and when this action will happen.

2. Spend 5 minutes at the start of each day jotting down what you are going to do that day to make progress toward one or more of your goals.

3. As you progress through each working day, constantly ask yourself "Is what I am doing right now moving me towards one of my long term goals?" Use Covey's Time Management Matrix to help you make decisions about what to do now, plan to do later or put off doing (perhaps entirely).

4. Every Friday morning, spend 10 minutes reviewing your progress toward your long term goals.

5. Repeat points 2, 3 & 4 for at least the next month.

Chapter 19

How to Manage your Email

How to manage your email. I almost can't believe I just wrote that – it's probably an oxymoron. "Managing" and "Emails" just don't seem to go together. Every manager I talk with, says that they get too many emails and they have difficulty managing them. Well, I've spoken with all the email management experts, read everything I can on the subject and analysed my own email habits. Here's my advice . . .

Process and Content – efficiency and effectiveness

This chapter is divided into two parts. Managing the process of sending and receiving emails is covered in the first part – these tips should add to your time management efficiency. The second part of the chapter focuses on content – what should and should not be put in emails. Good content management should add to the impact and ultimately, effectiveness of your emails.

Managing the Email Process

The underlying principle behind most of the following tips, is that to manage your email more efficiently, you also need to get others involved in helping you. Some of the tips will do this without the receiver noticing. However, for other tips, you will get the most impact if you tell people what you are doing and why. Get them to help you. Take the first tip for example . . .

1. **Decide on the best time of the day to do your emails and stick to it - make it your *Email Time***

Think for a moment about the time of day that you are at your most creative and brightest at work. Got it? Right, now make sure that this time is NOT used for emails. For two thirds of us, morning is when we are at our best and just after lunch is when we are at our least productive.

For the most part, emails do not require creativity nor intuitive thought. So, the best time to do your emails is straight after lunch. This leaves your mornings free for the creative and challenging managerial work that you need to do.

- If you use Outlook (or similar), change the default to open to your Calendar and Task List, rather than your Inbox
- Turn off the popup and reminder sound for advising when email comes in

Just doing these two things, will help you stick to your daily email time.

Keep in mind that paper mail only arrives once a day, why not make emails similar? Avoid the temptation to respond to each email as it comes in. Stick to your *email time.*

Remember, it's also a good idea to tell others, particularly people who email you regularly and your team, about your *email time.* This will get others started on helping you manage your emails more efficiently.

2. Block out a specific amount of time to process your emails

You should base this on how long it currently takes you to do your emails each day. Granted, the time will be somewhat different each day, depending on the number of emails. As a tool for better managing your emails, try to reduce this time by a certain amount each day, say 5 minutes, until you get to what you consider to be an efficient and effective amount of time to spend on your emails each day.

When you do process emails, try to spend a maximum of two minutes per email. This is just a guide, as some will take you a lot longer, but try to aim for it.

3. Take action on each email as you read it rather than read through your entire inbox

Scan the subject lines in your inbox. If there are related emails, take action on these first.

Otherwise, open each email as you come to it and take any necessary action. Try not to read through your entire inbox in detail before going back to take action on particular emails. This is very inefficient use of your time as you will only have to read them again when you want to take action. As you take emails one by one, take any necessary action straight away. This may mean:

- Responding to the sender immediately (preferable), or
- If your response only requires a small amount of side work, do it straight away, or
- If the email requires you to undertake a considerable amount of work, respond immediately advising when you will get back to the sender and put the work on your "To Do" list. Move on to the next email.

Handling each email in turn and doing something with it, helps to keep your inbox clear.

4. Keep your inbox clear

At the end of each day, make sure your inbox is clear and you are ready to start fresh tomorrow. Using your inbox as a filing system is not very efficient. By taking action on emails daily, you not only become more efficient, you feel good about your email management at the end of each day. (This tip has really worked well for me since I first wrote this chapter)

5. Phone some people instead of responding to their email

If the incoming email requires a discussion type response, try phoning the sender rather than emailing. You'll probably be surprised at how much more you will achieve through actually talking to the person. This also helps build your relationships with peers, colleagues, customers and so on (and perhaps helps show others that the phone still has its place).

It's a good idea to phone people if they are:

- On the same floor in the building as you
- In the same building

- Someone you have not actually spoken with for a while
- A person who usually takes a considerable time to respond to your emails

If you phone people occasionally, they are more likely to phone you when they have something to discuss rather than sending you an email.

By the way, do you have your phone number listed in the footer of your emails? If you want people to phone occasionally, they need to have easy access to your number.

6. Have an *Email Free* day

I can remember the time before emails and it wasn't that long ago. (Now, you're thinking "How old is Bob?") A very far sighted colleague of mine could see both the advantages and potential pitfalls of emails when they were introduced. At the time, he instituted his own email rule which he told everyone about - "I will only respond to your emails every Friday".

Could that rule still be valid today? Well, for him, it is. He is an extremely popular and successful consultant, so much so, that he has so much work he has to regularly pass on work to colleagues. So, how do people contact him? Guess what, they phone. And he's not overloaded with phone calls either. You might ask, "What's happening here?" What he's done is to train us, his colleagues, customers and others, to really think about "Why?" we want to contact him and "What?" our message will entail.

Now, it's probably a bit late for you and I to start a similar rule with our key people. However, there is a small but growing number of organisations around the world who have realised the loss of productivity caused by the over emphasis on emails. For example, to help overcome the problem, Scott A. Dockter, CEO of PBD Worldwide Fulfillment Services, has instituted a "No email Fridays" policy. He is reported to have told his employees to use the phone on Fridays for all their communication (internal and external) and to reduce email use the rest of the week. Not only has this reduced the reliance on emails and improved interpersonal communication, but in less than four months it also resulted in quicker problem solving, better teamwork and happier customers.

Why not start your own email free day?

7. Let other people know about your email management plans

As with all good intentions, if they are to be realised, you will need to involve others. You will be most aware of who you need to communicate your intentions to. However, at a minimum this should include your manager, team, peers and key customers/suppliers.

A final word or two on email process management ...

Keep in mind that you are in the business of your business, not in the business of emails. So if you are in service, production, research, sales, whatever – this is your real business. Emails should be nothing more than an incidental tool to help you achieve better results, they should not become the major part of your daily workload.

Managing the Content of your emails

What's the major problem with what we put in our emails? Well, before answering that, read the following statement:

"I did not say she stole the money"

Now read it aloud to yourself (doesn't matter if anyone else is around, they won't know what you're doing).

My question! What is the meaning of this statement? What did you interpret from this written statement?

Did you think that:

- *"**I**" did not say she stole the money..,* or that
- *I did "**NOT**" say she stole the money..,* or that
- *I did not "**SAY**" she stole the money ...,* or that
- *I did not say "**SHE**" stole the money ...,* or that
- *I did not say she "**STOLE**" the money,* or that
- *I did not say she stole the "**MONEY**"!*

Starting to get the picture? You see, whenever you put words on paper (or in this case in emails) they can be interpreted in many different ways – and often are. In fact the legal profession (with apologies to anyone of a legal nature reading this) have built an entire industry on the interpretation of the written word. Signed any contracts lately? Notice that they almost never have punctuations and even when they do, they can still be interpreted by two independent people, quite differently.

A recent study showed that up to 52% of the message in emails was misinterpreted due to the inability of the receiver to fully grasp the meaning of the intended message.

By now you may have guessed what the golden rule and first step in email content management, should be:

1. Restrict emails to reason and logic – send emotions face to face

If the message has any emotional intent or is likely to have an impact on the receiver's emotions, look for another way other than email to send it. Generally, this will mean face to face, or as a last resort, over the phone or by video hook up, video cam etc.

Emails should only be for fact, logic and reason. I have seen so many emails which appeared on the surface to be innocent, start a war of words between consenting adults that if it wasn't so serious, would almost be laughable. In fact, two colleagues who once had a very good relationship, eventually ended up in legal action over each other's interpretation of a simple email message.

Emails are unlike any other written word – they are not books, newspapers or such where a great deal of thought has gone into the written word (and which is often accompanied by a visual image). Nor are they read that way, but keep in mind, that they can be re-read by the receiver many times over (and even by people wishing to interpret your meaning in a court of law).

Often emails are written quickly and sometimes without review, yet they have replaced much of the face to face communication and phone communication that once made up so much of our interpersonal relationships. For example, how often do you see people sending emails to one another when they are in the office next door or at the next desk or cubicle, rather than speaking with the person directly?

Emails also lack all of the nonverbal communication that is going on all the time as we talk face to face with one another and which helps us understand each other. Numerous studies (e.g. Mehrabian and Ferris 1967) have suggested that in face to face communication, in terms of interpreting the message that is being sent by one person to another:

- 55-60% is through the non verbal signals that are being picked up
- 35-40% is through the tone of voice being used
- 7-10% is via the actual words that are spoken

Another recent survey disclosed that up to 37% of a first impression is based upon the speaker's tone of voice. On the telephone, that number rises to 80% or higher.

So, if you have a message that is meant to be motivational, assertive or in any way intended to impact the behaviour or feeling of the receiver, where does that leave you with only words, 7%, to play with?

As Tim Dowling put it "This makes email a unique medium. The lack of nonverbal clues makes it easy to misinterpret something, but we're not careful enough to avoid these misinterpretations because email feels so instant, easy and accessible, just like talking."

If you want to really influence someone's thinking or impact their behaviour, go and speak with the person face to face.

2. Avoid the "You" word in your emails

How do you avoid unintentionally impacting the receiver's feelings? By the way, using any amount of "smilies" or similar 'emoticons' at the bottom of your email, or as is creeping into emails at the moment, at the end of sentences, will have no positive effect – in fact they may even work against you. Some people detest them.

Other than being as courteous as possible and re-reading the message carefully before sending it, the main word to avoid in your message is

"You" – particularly when used to describe past behaviour. "I" messages v's "You" messages were discussed in detail in Chapter 7, "How to give feedback – positive and negative". Check out that chapter if you want to review this very important communication skill. However, it is such an important communication tool, that some further explanation and information are included here.

When used to describe past behaviour, "You" often infers blame for something that the receiver has or has not done. It's probably not intended this way, but that's what happens.

To make this point clearer, think for a moment about the last time you had a really heated argument with someone. What often triggers such arguments is one person inferring blame by using "You" too often. "You never do that for me", or "You always miss my appointments". Pretty soon the other person joins in with their own "You" and what started out as a genuine and positive conversation, deteriorates into an argument. My bet is that when you really think about your last argument you had, the word that was used more than any other, was "You" – and it was used to describe past behaviour.

Those of you who have done any assertiveness training will know that replacing "You" with "I" can be very powerful and without offending the other person. As a simple and quick exercise, rewrite the two "You" statements used earlier as "I" statements:

A poor blaming "You" statement ...	Could be better written as ...
"You never do that for me"	
"You always miss my appointments"	

3. Decide the intention of your email

Before you type anything into a new message, answer the following questions:

- Why am I writing this?
- What exactly do I want the result of this message to be? and perhaps,
- What do I want the receiver to do as a result of this message?

People get so many emails every day, that if you haven't clearly and precisely decided what you want from your message, then the receiver is likely to take less notice of it, or at worst delete it.

There are potentially three reasons for your email:

- To **provide information** - "John, our project deadline has been extended by five days."
- To **request information** - "When will we receive the feedback from the client?"
- To **request action** - "Will you please send a copy of our most recent proposal to Andrea?"

If you are clear on what you want from the email, then there's a good likelihood it will also be clear to your receiver.

4. Use the subject line to summarise the intent of your message

People often read through their emails by subject line before opening them. You need to grab the reader's attention:

- Make the subject line a summary of the intent of your message.
- Also, when you respond to an email, change the sender's subject line to reflect the intent of your response.

This simple technique of summarising your intent in the subject line does wonders for improving the impact of your emails. There's also an added advantage to having descriptive subject lines. Later, it is much easier to go back and find a specific email amongst many emails from the same person, when it has a very descriptive subject line.

Poor subject lines ...	Better subject lines ...
1. Invoices	1. July invoices for your approval
2. Re: Book publishing	2. Looking for publishing advice please
3. Re: Lunch	3. Can we meet for lunch to discuss Project X
4. Follow-up	4. Plans attached for part 2 of Project ABC
5. Information	5. Please supply a copy of Brochure ACZ

6. Give your reader full context at the start of your message

Set out the overview and context of your message in the first paragraph.

Poor opening paragraph ...	Better opening paragraph ...
I agree with your recommendations.	This note is to confirm our phone conversation and agreement reached yesterday. It is quite OK to use a different report format for this project.

Develop the right habits:

- Decide the intent of your email
- Use the subject line to summarise the intent of your message
- Set out the overview and context of your message in the first paragraph

These three techniques will have an enormous impact on the effectiveness of your emails.

7. When you copy or "cc" people, do so for a reason and tell them why

One of the things that annoy people most, is being copied on emails when there is really no need. Often this is done in the mistaken belief that the sender is communicating and including others in the communication. This just adds to other's inbox and instead of helping the copied person, annoys them. Perhaps another reason so many people are copied on emails is for use as an alibi in case something "slips through the cracks". People either need to be copied for a valid reason, or they don't. Make this an important decision when you send out emails.

Poor CC ...	Better CC ...
Cc... John Reid, Andrea Maken	Cc... John Reid, Andrea Maken
Subject: Training program completed successfully	**Subject:** Training program completed successfully
On Friday, we successfully completed the training for the 8 new Finance Managers ...	**JR:** DECISION NEEDED. How many will be included in the next intake? **AM:** PLEASE ADVISE. Which departments will be included in the new training? On Friday, we successfully completed the training for the 8 new Finance Managers -

After you carefully consider who should be copied, you may find it necessary to send someone a separate email instead. This may seem like a little extra work at the time. However, it will ultimately improve your communication and quite possibly, your decision making. If you do need to send someone a separate email, you may be able to save some time by copying and pasting from the original, then adding the specific information for this person.

8. Match your communication medium to the preferences of the receiver

Let's face it. Some people are chronically poor at responding to their emails for whatever reasons. If you know this to be the case, why send them an email and then get frustrated when they fail to respond within the time that you would like?

Phone the person, or go and see them if this is convenient.

Finally ...

Be careful of what you put into emails, remember, they can be read many times over, even in a court of law. Re-read and review each email before you send it. And most importantly, if you feel that it is likely to have an emotional impact, go and see the person, or at very least phone them.

HOW TO IMPLEMENT THE IDEAS IN THIS CHAPTER

☞ **How to start improving your Email Management straight away**

1. Make a commitment now, to make a change to the way you manage your emails.
2. Pick two of the following PROCESS management tips and two CONTENT management tips and implement these immediately.
3. Explain what you are doing so that people will be able to give you some feedback on the effectiveness of your plan.

To improve PROCESS management	To Improve CONTENT management
☐ Decide on the best time of the day to do your emails and stick to it! Make it your *Email Time*	☐ Restrict emails to reason and logic – send emotions face to face
☐ Block out a specific amount of time to process your emails	☐ Avoid the "You" word in your emails, particularly when describing past behaviour of the other person
☐ Action each email as you read it rather than read them all first	☐ Decide the intention of your email
☐ Keep your inbox clear – make sure it is clear at the end of the day	☐ Use the subject line to summarise the intent of your message
☐ Phone some people instead of responding to their email	☐ Give your reader full context at the start of your message in the first paragraph
☐ Have an *Email Free* day!	☐ When you copy or "CC" people, do so for a reason and tell them why
☐ Let other people know about your email management plans	☐ Match your communication medium to the preferences of the receiver

☞ **How to really improve your Email Management**

1. Organise a team meeting to discuss how your entire team could improve their emails.
2. Use the process discussed in Chapter 15 "How to get the best out of your meetings" to prepare and run the meeting. This will also give you some good practice at writing the "Pre-work Meeting Question".
3. Develop and agree an email management plan with your team.

Chapter 20

*Five of the Worst Mistakes New Managers Make and Five
Principles on How to Avoid Them*

Mistake # 1: Treating people as "resources" not people

Case 1: Jane

*Jane worked as a waitress in a classy café. Her boss would not allow her
or any of the other staff to talk to one another unless it was directly related to work. In fact if they did, they were often chastised in front of customers. As a further measure, he installed cameras supposedly for
security, but which were actually used to monitor staff interaction.*

*When Jane and her colleagues picked up their pay at the end of the week,
they were always lectured about what they had done wrong during the
week – there was never any praise. As you might expect, staff turnover
was very high.*

**Principle # 1: Treat staff as entire people, not merely work re-
sources (not even "human" resources)**

Work-life and life outside of work, cannot be separated – the
person is the same person, no matter where they are. As a
manager, you employ the entire person, not just their mind and body during working hours. In fact, it is probably because of who they are as an
entire person that you originally hired them.

It's often amazing what people can become if they are allowed to.
Chances are, that the most memorable restaurant experience you have
ever had was in a restaurant where people like Jane and her colleagues
were not treated as resources, but were allowed to be themselves, i.e. the
full person.

Encourage all of your people to be who they are – that's why you em-

251

ployed them.

Mistake # 2:   Not doing what you say you are going to do

You will probably recall the story of Rob from an earlier chapter. This is such an important principle that his story is repeated here.

Case 2: Rob

Rob worked as a qualified, but junior physiotherapist in a busy hospital. He along with three of his colleagues were asked by their manager to discuss amongst themselves how they would like their rosters to be organised (i.e. who would do what shifts etc.) and put forward their proposal.

Rob and his colleagues were very happy with their final roster choices as they had considered all of their personal and professional needs and felt that their decision was the best for all. A day before the new rosters were to start, Rob found out by rumour during his lunch break that their roster recommendations were not to be implemented. Worse still, the rosters decided on by their manager did not suit any of the four. This decision by their manager resulted in a severe lowering of morale within the team and created a culture of mistrust with management. In future, they would be very wary of any suggestion from management.

Principle # 2:   Do what you say you will do – "Walk the talk"

Just in case this message isn't as clear as I would like it to be, let me drive it in with a sledge hammer. Rob's manager had raised the expectations of the team by his request that they organise their own rosters. So far as the team was concerned, their boss had promised that their proposal would be implemented. Not implementing the proposal was seen as a broken promise.

Not only did the manager not do what he said he was going to do, but he also took away one of the key motivators - giving people responsibility for managing their own work.

Obviously, the manager started out the right way, but took back the responsibility very quickly. Keep in mind that once performance expectations have been set and agreed, giving people the responsibility as to how they will achieve these expectations can be highly motivating.

Above all, if you want to develop as a recognised leader and manager by your team, always try to do what you say you are going to do. If you can't fulfil on your intentions or promises, say so early on and explain why. Or as a good friend once said "Under promise and over deliver".

Mistake # 3:   Not setting ground rules and performance expectations

Can the "give people responsibility" motivator be taken too far?

Case 3: Emma

Emma, another professional person worked in a team with a very relaxed boss. Emma's manager gave everyone a lot of freedom in how they managed themselves and their work. For example, the manager introduced an informal "time in lieu" system that allowed people to take time off when they had worked extra hours without claiming overtime. On the surface, this sounded like a great idea and was popular with all the staff. However, one of Emma's colleagues started to abuse the system to the extent that she actually did private work within work hours that enabled her to build up her "time in lieu". Emma became very agitated and demotivated by the actions of her colleague.

What could Emma's manager have done to prevent this?

Principle # 3:   Set and agree the ground rules at the start of any new initiative

The key to ensuring a scheme like this works, is to cover all the bases at the start (and if it isn't realistic to cover all bases at the start, set a date for a review of how the new initiative is working and how it should be improved).

For example, when setting the ground rules for the scheme, ask the staff to consider and recommend:

- What should happen if one of our colleagues abuses the system?

- What will we say to both our colleague and our manager?
- What action should the manager take?"

Using this approach, the manager still holds true to the "Responsibility" motivating principle. The manager is ensuring that the staff take responsibility not only for their actions, but also for the consequences of their actions. Then, should a problem occur, the manager's role in fixing the problem is made much easier – in fact, often if the ground rules have been well worked out and agreed by all at the start, problems do not emerge.

Mistake # 4:   Not helping people develop to their full potential

Case 4: Andrew

Andrew was a long term (10 years) professional in a team of highly qualified people who were given the responsibility of managing their own work. People enjoyed their work, they enjoyed the freedom, they enjoyed the challenges their roles brought.

Andrew and his colleagues were highly motivated. They were highly respected by management. Andrew's manager was obviously good at managing the "Responsibility" principle – it was in another area of management that she suddenly (and unexpectedly) fell down.

Because of the challenging nature of the work and the range of experiences that were available within Andrew's team, management decided to send all the new graduate recruits to Andrew's manager for training and development. The manager grasped the opportunity and immediately started to give all the new recruits the most interesting and challenging work. The old timers such as Andrew, were relegated to the mundane. Within five months, six of the very experienced people had resigned.

Principle # 4:   Provide training, development and coaching for all your people

What went wrong within this once highly motivated team? Andrew's manager lost sight of one of the other five intrinsic motivators – "The opportunity for growth and development" - it has to be for everybody, not just the chosen few.

No matter how long a person has been in the role, they still look for opportunities to expand their self knowledge, skills and competencies – they need to be challenged. Andrew's manager certainly applied this to the new recruits, but forgot to keep applying it with her long term staff.

As a new manager yourself, it's very easy to focus on the needs of the new or less experienced team members. However, we sometimes forget that even the most experienced team members want and need further development.

Mistake # 5:   Not recognising people for their contribution

Case 5: Margaret

Margaret was one of a team of five people employed in a restaurant. Neither she, nor any of her colleagues were permitted to present the customer with the bill at the end of the meal – the manager insisted on doing this. The manager also collected payment from the customer and arranged change or credit card processing.

When Margaret first started working at the restaurant, she was told that the manager liked to personally thank every customer and so staff were not permitted to play any part in the payment process.

So, Margaret and her colleagues never saw the final customer's bill. However, tips were tallied by the manager and distributed evenly between Margaret and her colleagues and they seemed fair enough.

On the surface, this seems like a reasonable approach for the manager to take. After all, thanking the customers personally is good customer service and he is distributing the tips fairly.

Margaret enjoyed her interaction with the customers, but she never felt highly motivated nor fulfilled at the end of a shift.

So, if Margaret is being treated fairly, but still feels unfulfilled, where is the manager going wrong? What is the management principle that is being missed here?

Principle # 5:   Provide recognition for a job well done

Tips are a form of recognition from customers that they have received good service. To some extent and in some cultures, they are expected and indeed there may be a standard formula (10%, 15% etc). However, it's the "recognition" aspect of the tip, not the money, that's the motivating factor that's missing here. Not being able to see how the customers appreciated the service given by Margaret, nor hear the words of praise, led to Margaret's less than optimal motivation.

"Recognition for achievement" is one of the five intrinsic motivators. If recognition is not given, people tend to only perform to a certain standard that enables them to keep their job, not above and beyond what one would normally expect. Without recognition, they are unlikely to do their best work,

You will recall the importance of recognition from the chapter on "How to Motivate Others". This has been a major theme of the book and one that I really hope you take to heart as it really does work. However, you don't have to take my word for it. A recent study by Maritz, who have been conducting an annual poll of approximately 1,000 employees since 1988, found that:

"55 percent of employees agree or strongly agree that the quality of their company's recognition efforts impacts their job performance. At the same time, only 10 percent of employees strongly agree that they are completely satisfied with their company's recognition efforts".

Praise, the thing that motivates us the most, takes so little time and yet costs nothing! As the famous management writer Rosabeth Moss Kantor once said *"Compensation is a right. Recognition is a gift."*

HOW TO IMPLEMENT THE IDEAS IN THIS CHAPTER

☞ How to avoid some of the mistakes new managers make

Management Principle to Implement	Some tips for implementing . . .
1. **Treat staff as entire and whole people, not merely work resources**	• Get to know each of your people – what are their likes and dislikes? • How and when do they do their best work? • Who do they work well with?
2. **Do what you say you will do – "Walk the talk"**	• Be careful about promising too much – enthusiasm is good, but make it realistic • Keep a diary note to follow up on the important things you have said you will do for people and the team • If for some reason you can't fulfil on your intentions, say so and why
3. **Set and agree the ground rules at the start of any new initiative**	• When you and the team have agreed on a new initiative that will effect everyone, have a discussion and agree what could go wrong and how this should be managed
4. **Provide training, development and coaching for all your people**	• Ask people what training or coaching they might need • Rotate people through various jobs / roles / tasks (this is not always easy, but if it is at all possible it should be tried). • Read the introduction to this book again – apply some of the learning ideas to the different people in your team
5. **Provide recognition for a job well done**	• Make a point to recognize and praise someone every day for something they have achieved • Be genuine with your praise

Chapter 21

How to Develop Yourself to Your Full Potential

Are you positive or negative?

Some years ago, I read a report by Spiro Zavos in the sports columns of my Sydney Morning Herald newspaper, which described the behaviour of a football coach during a very tense finals game. The antics of the losing coach gave a very good insight into why his team did not win and in fact loses many close games. In part, Zavos' report read:

"He was at his over-emotional worst at Lancaster Park on Sunday. The eyes rolled more wildly than ever, he stalked the sideline. Not even the television cameras were safe from his flaying arms. His antics sent a damaging message to his team: that the fates are conspiring against them and they are, somehow, destined to lose. And for the second week in a row they lost a critical game."

The winning coach on the other hand: *" ... sat impassively in the stands. The sign he gave to his players with this emotionless posture was that if the players wanted to win, they had to do it themselves. And they did. Just."*

Both these coaches were very experienced and knowledgeable about the game. Both had got their teams to the finals. But why did one coach's team always lose the close games and the other always win?

It all has to do with the positive or negative outlook we have. This outlook can dramatically impact both our own behaviour and that of those around us.

Often we are not aware of the messages we are sending through our actions. Psychologists call this a Locus of Control (first developed by

258

Julian Rotter, 1966). Locus of Control refers to a person's perception of the main causes of the events in their life. For example;

- Do you believe that your destiny is controlled by yourself? - "I did it myself" or,
- Controlled by external forces such as fate or other people? - "It was their fault"

What's your Locus of Control?

Put simply, if you believe that your behaviour is guided by your personal decisions and efforts, then you are said to be more internally focused, i.e. you have an internal locus of control. On the other hand, if you believe that your behaviour is guided by fate, luck, or other external circumstances, then you are said to have an external locus of control.

Is one better than the other? That's always the $64,000 question in psychology. Generally, people with an internal locus of control tend to have greater influence on their motivation, expectations, self-esteem, risk-taking behaviour, and even on the actual outcome of their actions. As you would expect, some studies also suggest that people with an internal locus of control tend to be more positive in their behaviour and outlook.

Can you tell what your locus of control is? Perhaps the people who know you well can answer this best for you. There is also a number of short tests freely available on the web that you can take. These only take a few minutes to complete and will give you a good guide.

The second, and probably more important question is;

- if you decide that you need to be more internally focused, can you change your locus of control?

The answer is an unequivocal, "Yes".

Many studies have shown that our locus of control is a learned behaviour and as such, can be changed. My own experience in working as a coach to club, national and international rowing coaches, confirms this. I was able to train coaches to improve their internal focus by getting them to change the behaviour they used with their athletes. The athletes, myself and the coaches themselves, were able to discern a far greater positive outlook by the coaches within 12 months.

This approach has also been successful in my role as a training consultant. Working with new and aspiring managers who were keen to improve the motivation of their team, I first had the managers look at themselves and improve their locus of control, before looking at their team. Most often, team motivation increased as a direct result of the changed behaviour of the manager, not by any action by the team.

How does Locus of Control relate to personal development?

Hopefully by this point, you have decided that your own development starts with you. As you are reading this book, there is a very good chance that you already have an internal locus of control and a positive outlook. Because of this positive outlook you have, it is also most likely that you want to become even more positive and better at what you do. (I find that it's often the people who least need the type of development outlined in this book, who have the capacity to benefit most from it)

How can I improve my outlook?

How do you change your locus of control and consequently your outlook? There are a number of training programs available that use effective behavioural change methods to help move people from a more external focus to a more internal focus. But, if you want a very simple method that you can start applying straight away, then changing the words you use in everyday conversations can have a major impact.

Use positive language

For instance, getting rid of the word "don't" from your vocabulary and replacing it with the positive image of what you are suggesting, starts to make you far more positive in your outlook. Take a look at the following short statements. What do you actually visualise as you read each one?

- *Don't drop it!*
- *Don't walk on the grass.*
- *In case of fire do not use lifts (elevators).*

"Don't drop it!" The only image we see in our brain when someone says that to us, is the picture of "I'm dropping this". It's also likely that at the same time we think about the negative consequences of dropping something. Thinking about the negative consequences of dropping something probably goes back to our childhood, when we got into trouble for "dropping it".

"Don't walk on the grass". The image this conjures up in our brain is of a person actually walking on the grass, not the footpath as the message intends. "Footpath" is never mentioned, so why would we have an image in our mind of staying on the footpath (which is what we should be doing)?

"In case of fire do not use lifts". In this example, the only thing we can visualise is the lift (elevator). In fact, studies have shown that when there is a fire emergency and the vestibule or foyer starts to fill with smoke, the only word that people recognise on these types of signs, is "lift". The result? When under threat of imminent danger, people immediately head straight for the lift and not the emergency exit as was intended. Some authorities have now changed their signage to read "In case of fire, use the emergency exit pictured in this diagram". Notice that in this new example the word "lift" is not used at all. And in addition the words "emergency exit" have now been supported by the visual diagram of exactly where the exits are located.

Start to get the picture? Any words that follow the word "don't" in a statement or on a sign, are what we visualise. Each of the original "don't" statements mentioned above, immediately has both the sender and the receiver visualising and thinking of exactly the opposite, negative action - not the action that was intended and should be taken.

By eliminating the word "don't" and replacing it with the positive action you intend, you will now start to think and subsequently behave, more positively. Additionally, your positive words and behaviour will impact your audience more positively. Because you are now taking responsibility for the positive actions you expect of others, rather than the negative, you also start to become more internally focused.

As an example, look at the way a person with an internal locus of con-

261

trol, might express the three negative statements mentioned earlier …

- *"Don't drop it!"* is expressed as *"Hold on to the glass very carefully"*
- *"Don't walk on the grass"* is expressed as *"Walk on the footpath"*
- *"In case of fire do not use lift"* is expressed as *"In case of fire use the fire exit described in the following diagram"*

In these new statements, both the sender and the receiver get the positive message immediately.

These three examples also show how culturally ingrained these "Don't" statements are. It takes a conscious act of will to turn them around and become positive.

Can this technique of eliminating the word "Don't" work for you?

Twelve months after the start of their training, I did some follow up interviews with the athletes of the rowing coaches I had been training. Without exception, the athletes all expressed the theme that "She has really changed over the last 12 months. We are not sure what you included in your training with our coach, but she is so much more positive these days. We really enjoy being coached by her".

Is it easy to replace "don't" with a positive image? In theory, yes. But in my own case, it took me about 12 months. Occasionally, I still find myself using a "don't", but when I do, an alarm bell goes off in my brain and I immediately rephrase my statement to the positive image I want to get across. As a result, over the last few years, people have commented to me "Bob, you seem to be such a positive person. Even when you are faced with adversity or a real problem, you always seem to take a positive approach. I really enjoy working with you".

So, the starting point for your personal development and growth is to check your Locus of Control. There's also something else you need to check, your behaviour.

Where are you now?

What have you done since starting to read this book? Have you undertaken any of the other development activities? Many of them have been designed not only to help you straight away as a new manager, but also to develop your managerial skills over the longer term and ultimately, your future career.

However, the real starting point for self-development, as with any other developmental activity, is to benchmark your current status as a manager. What are your strengths and weaknesses? Are you accurately aware of these? Test yourself. In the following table, list the three key strengths and three major weaknesses you believe you have as a manager:

My three key STRENGTHS as a manager are:	My three major WEAKNESSES as a manager are:
•	•
•	•
•	•

For example in my own case they are:

My three key STRENGTHS as a manager are:	My three major WEAKNESSES as a manager are:
• A good listener – can help people solve their issues or problems well	• Not good at handling strongly opinionated or powerful managers
• A creative presenter and writer – can usually come up with an innovative and workable way of solving an issue or problem	• Not good at giving negative feedback – can spot poor performance easily, but unwilling to tell the person at the time
• Ability to perform under pressure – when deadlines are tough, will always come through on time	• Can sometimes procrastinate so that important work is left to the last minute

It probably goes without saying, that it is important to know what your strengths and weaknesses are. However, research into management and leadership effectiveness over the last 10 years has also consistently found that:

- Managers who **regularly seek and get feedback** on their performance, are amongst the **better performing managers.**

263

- Managers who are **accurately aware** of their own strengths and weaknesses are seen as **better leaders.**

These are two pretty powerful reasons for getting some feedback about your strengths and weaknesses.

Getting accurate feedback

Now, finding out "How am I doing?" has always been a thorny issue for many managers. It's relatively easy to get feedback on your actual results, the task part of your job, for example sales, production targets, budgets etc. But it becomes more difficult to get feedback on how you manage others – i.e. the behaviours you use, the relationship part of your job. Often the only feedback you get is when your boss tells you that "something has gone wrong". Or, when perhaps you do get some feedback from colleagues, it is often very general and likely to be of a more positive nature.

Rather than waiting for this spasmodic feedback, there is a better way you can develop an accurate view of your strengths and weaknesses. You can actively seek feedback on how you are seen by others, from others. You should then compare this feedback to your self perception.

You can do this by:

- Formally asking people who know you, such as peers, colleagues, team members, even spouses / partners. The downside of this approach is that people may not be as honest as they should be for fear of hurting you. You can improve this process by giving the blank table above to some of your feedback people and asking them to list three things in each column.
- Getting more formal feedback through a process such as a 360 degree feedback profile. This will undoubtedly improve both the honesty and accuracy of the feedback.

What's 360° Feedback?

Some years ago, the 360 degree feedback process was designed to overcome many of the inadequacies encountered with informal feedback. It's called "360' because feedback is sought in a structured way from:

- Your manager
- Your peers
- The people that report to you
- And you complete a "self" rating for comparison with the feedback of others.

In other words, a 360 degree view of your performance such as . . .

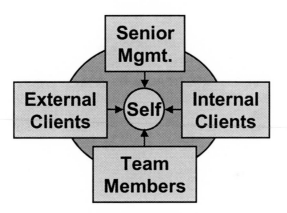

The process usually involves each person completing a questionnaire that asks how often do you exhibit common managerial behaviours? Often the responses are on a five point scale such as – always, often, occasionally, seldom or never?

The better 360° processes, also ask each of the people giving you feedback to add whether they would like to see you display "more" of each behaviour, the "same" amount, or "less" of each of the behaviours. In this way you can gain some meaningful and useful feedback that will assist with your development.

Draw up a Personal Development Plan for the next 12 months

Armed with an accurate assessment of your strengths and weaknesses, you can now put in place a plan for your own development:

- The plan should cover a period of 12 months so that you can really start to see results.
- The plan should include actions that both:
  - build on your strengths and make sure that these are maintained
  - provide strategies for overcoming or covering for, your weaknesses.
- Each action should have a completion time.
- You should discuss this plan with someone. Probably the best person would be your manager, or perhaps a trusted colleague. The reason for discussing the plan is that it is more likely to be implemented when you add the responsibility of reporting results to another person.

Remember,

- Managers who **regularly seek and get feedback** on their performance, are amongst the **better performing managers.**
- Managers who are **accurately aware** of their own strengths and weaknesses are seen as **better leaders.**

HOW TO IMPLEMENT THE IDEAS IN THIS CHAPTER

 How to start your development, straight away

1. Start using positive language when you ask someone to do something for you. Drop the use of the word "don't" from your vocabulary.

2. Ask some people who know you to complete the following table:

My three key STRENGTHS as a manager are:	My three major WEAKNESSES as a manager are:
•	•
•	•
•	•

3. Pick out ONE of your strengths and make sure you focus on applying this over the next three weeks.

4. Pick out ONE of your weaknesses:
    -   Talk with a trusted colleague
    -   Ask him/her what you could do to improve this behaviour
    -   Make sure you focus on applying this improvement suggestion consistently over the next three weeks
    -   Ask your colleague for feedback on your progress at the end of the three week period.

 How to develop yourself to your full potential!

1. Complete a "Locus of Control" questionnaire. Work on using positive language. Eliminate the word "don't" from your vocabulary.
2. Arrange to have a 360 degree profile completed.
3. Draw up a 12 month development plan along the following lines.

DEVELOPMENT PLAN - Phase 1: Analysis.

BEHAVIOURS LISTED IN THE 360° QUESTIONNAIRE	STRENGTHS	WEAKNESSES
For example ... **Leading Self & Others**		
For example ... **Leading – Building Relationships**		
For example ... **Leading – Communicating with Impact**		

DEVELOPMENT PLAN - Phase 2: Planning.

Areas of performance I wish to maintain, reinforce or develop	Actions I will take (and record in my diary where appropriate)	Checkpoint dates to assess progress	Performance Indicators - How I will know my plan is succeeding	Key people I will need to tell/involve if my plan is to be successful

4. Discuss this plan with your manager. Agree check point dates.
5. Discuss your plan with your mentor. Seek his / her advice.
6. Complete the 360 degree process again at the end of the 12 month period to assess your development.

Chapter 22

How to Develop Your Image, Your Persona

Do first impressions count?

I once worked with a young bloke named Neil. Neil was bright, energetic and well presented. There was only one detracting feature about Neil when you first met him – his handshake. Shaking hands with Neil was like holding a wet fish – limp and squashy. My boss at the time, Kendall (whom I mentioned earlier in the chapter on Appraisals) was a very perceptive person. Realising that in our business one had to make a good first impression, Kendall took Neil aside very soon after Neil started in the department for a chat.

I'm told the conversation went something along these lines …

"Neil, I can see that you have a lot of potential and you present yourself very well. There's only one detracting feature and that's your handshake. People make judgments about others when they first meet. One of the factors that influences their judgment is the handshake. I'd like to see you develop a much firmer handshake. Here's what I propose. Every morning when you come into my office to say 'Good Morning boss', I'd like us to shake hands. I want you to keep doing this every day until I tell you that you've got it right."

Many years later, well after I had moved on from that department, I met Neil in the street. And as old colleagues do, we shook hands. Well, he practically ripped my arm off! Either Neil had kept practising all these years or Kendall forgot to tell him when to stop, I'm not sure which, but the difference was amazing.

During our discussion, I discovered that Neil was now manager of the department. Can you put that meteoric rise down to first impressions?

Obviously not. Would he have made it without the handshake? Who knows. But, and I need to stress this, one's image or persona does have a major impact on how others evaluate you, both immediately and over the longer term.

There has been a tremendous amount of research done over the years on first impressions. This research consistently shows that:

- It takes less than 3 seconds to evaluate the other person based on their appearance, body language, demeanour, mannerisms and dress. And we do.
- These first impressions are extremely difficult to change or undo.
- Once people have made a judgment about the other person, they instinctively look for other clues (as the relationship progresses) to support their initial judgment. This is often referred to as the "halo effect".

In a recent Canadian study, researchers also found that it takes less than a 20th of a second for someone to make up their mind about the quality of a web page. So it seems, whether it's people or things, we make judgments almost as quickly as the eye can take in information.

What's your image? What do you want it to be in the eyes of others?

As a boy spending time on my uncle's farm, I learnt very early in life the value of image. Whenever there was a new salesman calling at the farm, my uncle would give me a running commentary on what to expect as the car came up the long drive. If the car was too new, then my uncle would say "Flashy, doesn't understand his customers, probably a young upstart from the city". If it was old and seen better days, he would say "Probably not very successful, maybe another farmer down on his luck and changing careers". After the salesmen had gone, he would ask me what I thought of them – the way they looked, dressed, mannerisms, did they speak to me? Invariably, his initial impressions seemed to me to be spot on.

You can make the image that you want

I once worked in a financial services organisation where there was a highly respected and successful internal auditor by the name of Charlie.

Charlie was an unusual dresser for an auditor. To start with he was very tall and thin – this could have been overpowering, but he had an uncanny knack of smiling at the right time. I also got the impression that with his piercing eyes, he could see right through you – he could certainly tell if you were lying. There was another unusual feature about Charlie. He wore the most outrageous shirts, and sticking out of the top of his shirt pocket you could see three pens; green, red and purple – these were the colours of auditors.

Think about Charlie's persona for a moment (even his name – I'm sure it was "Charles", but he had deliberately made it "Charlie"). What was he trying to portray?

What are some of the requirements of an internal auditor? An internal auditor needs to be a cross between a policeman and a counsellor – to be able to detect any improprieties as well as counsel staff on legal, ac-counting, ethical and if need be, personal matters. Charlie had deliber-ately set out to create an image that said; "I am an expert auditor, I see things that need to be seen. I'm also a warm and understanding person, I can handle feelings and emotional people".

How to identify the image for your organisation . . .

As a new manager, what's the image that you need to create? Take a look around the organisation – who are the three or four most admired and successful managers? Now, you want to emulate these people (not copy). How do you do this?

- Take four plain post-it note size cards.
- Write the four manager's names, one per card.
- Place the cards, name down, shuffle and draw two at random.
- On a sheet of paper, list the things about these two managers that are similar.
- Repeat the drawing of two cards and listing their likenesses until all combinations for the four managers have been exhausted.

You now have a list of traits, characteristics, behaviours, mannerisms, skills etc. that characterise these successful managers. In fact, you have just defined the key aspects of your successful role model's images. Let me repeat. You should not copy these people, but you can adapt your presentation, style, communication and ultimately your image, to match

271

that of the most successful managers in your organisation. After all, they've learnt what works, why not use their experience?

Can You Do It?

Are you in the business of adapting to the environment you find yourself in, or are you in the self-entertainment business? Many people will say "I am what I am, and if the organisation and its people don't like me the way I am, that's their problem." Well, maybe it is if you are the genius the organisation really cannot survive without. But if you are a normal competent person and your intention is to make a career in that organisation, it's not their problem – it's yours.

Can you project an image that will lead to success in the organisation and still be true to yourself? If you can't, you're in the wrong organisation and it's time to start looking for a new job. You need to make that important decision, so that you can move on and be successful either where you are or somewhere else.

How to display your image

Now that you have an idea of what your image should look like, here are some practical tips for displaying that image.

Tips for displaying your image . . .

1. **Dress to suit the organisation or the situation.** People do make judgments on what you wear, so make sure it's appropriate for the environment. Even when there are recognised casual days (or your organisation dresses casually) make sure your dress is smart and looks professional. I was sitting in the Head Office foyer of a major bank one Friday recently and it was obviously "casual" day. It was interesting to watch the staff coming and going. They were all dressed casually, but you could tell very easily those who cared about their appearance and those who did not. As Lord Chamberlain is reported to have said to his son "Dress is a very foolish thing; and yet it is a very foolish thing for a man not to be well-dressed."

2. **Learn and use people's names quickly.** One of the greatest compliments one can receive, is to be called by name. It's also very impressive when you can remember other people's names. Write them down as soon as you can, or if you don't have that immediate opportunity, repeat the person's name two or three times in the first few minutes of the conversation.

3. **Ask lots of questions and ask for help.** Asking questions shows a genuine interest in people. Asking for their help shows that you respect them – it also shows that you

---

are human and ready to learn.

4. **Listen more than talk.** Although people will want to hear your opinion, there's a fine line between giving your opinion and being over bearing. Err on the side of caution. Listen. It's amazing how much you will learn.

5. **Give praise and recognition.** Show your appreciation for the things people do for you. Compliment them on their good work.

You can learn to make a positive and lasting first impression, modify it to suit any situation, and come out a winner. It means that you need to think about what image you wish to portray and most importantly, "How will I present myself in this situation?"

HOW TO IMPLEMENT THE IDEAS IN THIS CHAPTER

↩ How to start building your image straight away

1. Undertake the following "successful manager" exercise.

2. Take a look around the organisation – who are the three or four most admired and successful managers? Now, you want to emulate these people (not copy). To do this:
   - Take four plain post-it note size cards.
   - Write the four manager's names, one per card.
   - Place the cards, name down, shuffle and draw two at random.
   - On a sheet of paper, list the things about these two managers that are similar.
   - Repeat the drawing of two cards and listing their likenesses until all combinations for the four managers have been exhausted.

3. Decide how these manager's persona differ from yours. Make a commitment to develop your skills in some of the areas that you have identified.

How to really develop your image

Steps to take . . .	Ideas to consider . . .
1. Complete the *Successful Manager* exercise	• Undertake as described above.
2. Ask a trusted colleague (mentor or coach) for assistance	• Ask him/her to identify the most successful managers in the organisation. • Ask: How do I differ from them? • Ask: How am I similar to them? • Add this information to that gleaned from the Successful Manager exercise and make the necessary changes.
3. Ask your current manager for assistance	• Once you are comfortable with the development of your image, ask your current manager to do the Successful Manager exercise with you. Take on board any of his/her pertinent comments.

Acknowledgements

Where does one start with all the people to thank for this book? Without the help of the following, this book would not have been possible.

Firstly, to my wife Anita, who has encouraged and helped me to get this far – my greatest fan, thank you so much.

To Dennis Pratt who has been through every word and every line of the manuscript and whose helpful comments and advice have added tremendously to the final product. I also owe a great debt of gratitude to Dennis for providing me with many of the original ideas and concepts that I have been able to apply and refine throughout my years as a manager and consultant.

To Peter Burleigh for his great artwork and for being a creative influence on me as a business partner for twelve years. I trust my writing style reflects your coaching Peter. And to Judi, who is always looking for "the" book.

To Humphrey Armstrong and Philip Rutledge who gave me some great comments on the original draft both in concept and writing style.

Also thank you to Catherine Owen whose experiences of being managed appear in the chapter on "Mistakes that new managers make" – I believe story telling is a great way to get a message across and what better way than from someone who has recently experienced some of the mistakes we managers make.

To the best team - John Nolan, Marcia Grant, Maree Day and Willy Limjap, and to John and Maree for their input to the chapter on "Teams".

Thanks also to Margaret Clark who looks after things for me in Sydney so well when I'm away in Switzerland and who always has the question that needs an answer.

And thanks also to the people who were kind enough to read the original manuscript and add their comments – Martin John, Humphrey Armstrong, Maria-Jose Campos and Luciano Almeida de Jesus.

And of course a big thank you to those of you reading this who have bought a copy – I trust that you have been able to benefit from some of the many ideas and concepts for getting things done through people.

References

American Judicature Society (2002), http://www.ajs.org/jc/juries/jc_decision_research.asp

Ashkenas, R.N. and Schaffer R.H. "Managers Can Avoid Wasting Time", Harvard Business Review, Feb 2002.

Belbin Team Roles. Belbin Associates. http://www.belbin.com/

Betten, N. and Austin, M. (1990) *The Roots of Community Organizing: 1917 - 1939*, Philadelphia: Temple University Press.

Covey, Stephen. Seven Habits of Highly Effective People. Simon & Schuster New York 1990.

Decision Preference Analysis – a selection tool. N.I.S. PO Box 74, Kenmore Qld 4069, Australia

Ferrazzi, K. Never Eat Alone: And Other Secrets to Success, One Relationship at a Time, Currency 2005

Herzberg, F. "One More Time; How do you Motivate Employees?" Harvard Business Review, Jan 2003.

Honey, Peter and Munford, Alan, Learning Preferences, www.peterhoney.com

Kanter, R.M. The Change Masters. George Allen & Unwin, London. 1983

Law Reform Commission of NSW (2001), http://www.ajs.org/jc/juries/jc_decision_research.asp

Lindahl, L. Foreman Facts, Labor Relations Institute of NY. Personnel Magazine 1949

Lindenberger, J. Truth or Consequence? How To Give Employee Feedback. http://www.lindenbergergroup.com/art_common.html

Maritz study (undated) St. Louis, USA. "Bosses not 'on the same page' as employees regarding recognition."

Mehrabian, Albert and Ferris, Susan R. "Inference of attitudes from nonverbal communication in two channels." Journal of Consulting Psychology 31 (1967): 248-252. and Susan R. Ferris, "Inference of attitudes from nonverbal communication in two channels."

Journal of Consulting Psychology 31 (1967): 248-252.

Oncken, W. and Wass, D. "Management Time: Who's got the Monkey", Harvard Business Review, Nov. 1999.

Pratt, D. Aspiring to Greatness: Above and Beyond Total Quality Management.

Robbins, S. Tips for Mastering E-mail Overload, HBR 10/25/2004

Rotter, J. B. Generalized expectancies for internal versus external control of reinforcement. Psychological Monographs, 80. 1966.

Saunders, S.A. Navigating in The New World. Ian Newcombe 2007.

Silberman, M. "Influencing Others the People-Smart Way" #567 Innovative Leader, Volume 11, Number 12, December 2002

Snyder, C. R.; Cowles, Chris; Impact of Positive and Negative Feedback Based on Personality and Intellectual Assessment., Journal of Consulting and Clinical Psychology, v47 n1 p207-09 Feb 1979

Team Management Profile. Team Management Systems. http://www.tms.com.au/tms03.html

van Vlooten, Dick, "Network Your Way Into Work", ScienceCareer.org

Vroom, V.H. and Yetton, P.W. (1973). *Leadership and decision-making*. Pittsburg: University of Pittsburg Press

Wellman, B.; Frank, K; "Network capital in a multi-level world: Getting support from personal communities." Social Capital: Theory and Research, N. Lin, K. Cook, R. Burt, Eds. (Aldine DeGruyter, Chicago, 2001), pp. 233-273.

Whitmore, J. Coaching for Performance: Growing People, Performance and Purpose. Nicholas Brealey Publishing. London 2002

Zeff, Lawrence E. and Higby, Mary A. Teaching More Than You Know. Academic Exchange Quarterly. Fall 2002. Volume 6, Issue 3.

About the Author

Bob Selden is a student of behaviour. He believes that the words and language we use not only impact our relationships with others, but also the way in which we behave. Recent research tends to support this belief. For example, studies at the Universities of Heidelberg, Neuchatel and Zurich (2007) show that when young male drivers hear male type words (such as "tough" and "rough") they automatically increase their speed, whilst hearing female type words (such as "pink" and "lipstick") leads to a reduction in their speed. Likewise, can the words a manager uses impact both his or her people relationships and behaviour? What To Do When You Become The Boss enables Bob to illustrate how this concept can help managers improve both their effectiveness and relationships with critical stakeholders. It also provides the opportunity for Bob to pass on many of the management models, theories and practical tips that he has picked up over a long and varied management career.

Bob Selden survived his first new manager's role in banking to eventually develop into a senior manager responsible for the career development of hundreds of other managers. During this growing process, and later as an organisational development consultant, trainer and coach, he learnt what works and what doesn't work when managing others. What To Do When You Become The Boss is the result of his learning which he is determined to pass on to help other new managers during their initial growth spurt.

Bob is an Australian who currently lives in Liestal Switzerland with his wife Anita, a senior manager in a large multinational organisation. As well as consulting to various organisations, he coaches on the Mobilizing People program at the International Institute for Management Development in Lausanne, Switzerland. Bob also facilitates on programs such as the Middle Manager Development program at the Australian Graduate School of Management in Sydney, Australia.

CPSIA information can be obtained at www.ICGtesting.com
Printed in the USA
BVOW070630060112

279924BV00003B/2/A